MAR - 8 1988

Modern Critical Interpretations

D. H. Lawrence's
Women in Love

Modern Critical Interpretations

The Oresteia
Beowulf
The General Prologue to
   The Canterbury Tales
The Pardoner's Tale
The Knight's Tale
The Divine Comedy
Exodus
Genesis
The Gospels
The Iliad
The Book of Job
Volpone
Doctor Faustus
The Revelation of St.
   John the Divine
The Song of Songs
Oedipus Rex
The Aeneid
The Duchess of Malfi
Antony and Cleopatra
As You Like It
Coriolanus
Hamlet
Henry IV, Part I
Henry IV, Part II
Henry V
Julius Caesar
King Lear
Macbeth
Measure for Measure
The Merchant of Venice
A Midsummer Night's
   Dream
Much Ado About
   Nothing
Othello
Richard II
Richard III
The Sonnets
Taming of the Shrew
The Tempest
Twelfth Night
The Winter's Tale
Emma
Mansfield Park
Pride and Prejudice
The Life of Samuel
   Johnson
Moll Flanders
Robinson Crusoe
Tom Jones
The Beggar's Opera
Gray's Elegy
Paradise Lost
The Rape of the Lock
Tristram Shandy
Gulliver's Travels

Evelina
The Marriage of Heaven
   and Hell
Songs of Innocence and
   Experience
Jane Eyre
Wuthering Heights
Don Juan
The Rime of the Ancient
   Mariner
Bleak House
David Copperfield
Hard Times
A Tale of Two Cities
Middlemarch
The Mill on the Floss
Jude the Obscure
The Mayor of
   Casterbridge
The Return of the Native
Tess of the D'Urbervilles
The Odes of Keats
Frankenstein
Vanity Fair
Barchester Towers
The Prelude
The Red Badge of
   Courage
The Scarlet Letter
The Ambassadors
Daisy Miller, The Turn
   of the Screw, and
   Other Tales
The Portrait of a Lady
Billy Budd, Benito Cer-
   eno, Bartleby the Scriv-
   ener, and Other Tales
Moby-Dick
The Tales of Poe
Walden
Adventures of
   Huckleberry Finn
The Life of Frederick
   Douglass
Heart of Darkness
Lord Jim
Nostromo
A Passage to India
Dubliners
A Portrait of the Artist as
   a Young Man
Ulysses
Kim
The Rainbow
Sons and Lovers
Women in Love
1984
Major Barbara

Man and Superman
Pygmalion
St. Joan
The Playboy of the
   Western World
The Importance of Being
   Earnest
Mrs. Dalloway
To the Lighthouse
My Antonia
An American Tragedy
Murder in the Cathedral
The Waste Land
Absalom, Absalom!
Light in August
Sanctuary
The Sound and the Fury
The Great Gatsby
A Farewell to Arms
The Sun Also Rises
Arrowsmith
Lolita
The Iceman Cometh
Long Day's Journey Into
   Night
The Grapes of Wrath
Miss Lonelyhearts
The Glass Menagerie
A Streetcar Named
   Desire
Their Eyes Were
   Watching God
Native Son
Waiting for Godot
Herzog
All My Sons
Death of a Salesman
Gravity's Rainbow
All the King's Men
The Left Hand of
   Darkness
The Brothers Karamazov
Crime and Punishment
Madame Bovary
The Interpretation of
   Dreams
The Castle
The Metamorphosis
The Trial
Man's Fate
The Magic Mountain
Montaigne's Essays
Remembrance of Things
   Past
The Red and the Black
Anna Karenina
War and Peace

These and other titles in preparation

Modern Critical Interpretations

D. H. Lawrence's
Women in Love

Edited and with an introduction by

Harold Bloom
Sterling Professor of the Humanities
Yale University

Chelsea House Publishers ◇ *1988*
NEW YORK ◇ NEW HAVEN ◇ PHILADELPHIA

© 1988 by Chelsea House Publishers,
a division of Chelsea House Educational Communications, Inc.,
  95 Madison Avenue, New York, NY 10016
  345 Whitney Avenue, New Haven, CT 06511
  5068B West Chester Pike, Edgemont, PA 19028

Introduction © 1988 by Harold Bloom

Printed and bound in the United States of America

10 9 8 7 6 5 4 3 2 1

∞ The paper used in this publication meets the minimum
requirements of the American National Standard for Permanence
of Paper for Printed Library Materials, Z39.48-1984.

Library of Congress Cataloging-in-Publication Data
D.H. Lawrence's Women in love.
  (Modern critical interpretations)
  Bibliography: p.
  Includes index.
  Summary: Selections of literary criticisms on
Lawrence's novel "Women in Love."
  1. Lawrence, D. H. (David Herbert), 1885–1930.
Women in Love. [1. Lawrence, D.H. (David Herbert),
1885–1930. Women in Love. 2. English literature—
History and criticism] I. Bloom, Harold. II. Series.
PR6023.A93W648   1988   823'.912   87–11790
ISBN 1–55546–025–9 (alk. paper)

Contents

Editor's Note

This book brings together a representative selection of the best modern critical interpretations of D. H. Lawrence's great novel, *Women in Love*. The critical essays are reprinted here in the chronological order of their original publication. I am grateful to Dennis Fawcett for his labor as a researcher for this volume.

My introduction centers upon Lawrence's apocalyptic vitalism, which is the psychic basis for *Women in Love*. H. M. Daleski begins the chronological sequence with his classic account of Birkin's and Ursula's mutual quest to liberate the self from death–in–life.

The relation between conscious and unconscious knowledge in the novel is expounded by Peter K. Garrett, after which Robert L. Caserio traces Lawrence's impulse towards fatherhood as a crucial hidden factor in "the family plot" of *Women in Love*.

Lawrence's hatred of the ideology of his society is seen as vital to the dynamics of *Women in Love* by John Worthen, while Gavriel Ben-Ephraim finds the novel to be a "bleak apocalypse" because of the consequence of the warring wills of Gerald and Gudrun. In Baruch Hochman's reading, that ruinous strife of lovers ensues from the shape the self takes in Lawrence, antithetically demanding both absolute solitude and total connectedness to another self.

The precarious rhythm of the relationship between Birkin and Ursula is analyzed by Philip M. Weinstein, who contrasts its hurt vitality to the deathliness of the union of Gerald and Gudrun. In this book's final essay, Maria DiBattista sums up *Women in Love* as the "Judgment Book" of Lawrence's reluctant apocalypse, his inconclusive struggle with a narrative form that could not present his full vision of the possibilities of human desire.

Introduction

Lawrence, hardly a libertine, had the radically Protestant sensibility of Milton, Shelley, Browning, Hardy—none of them Eliotic favorites. To say that Lawrence was more a Puritan than Milton is only to state what is now finely obvious. What Lawrence shares with Milton is an intense exaltation of unfallen human sexuality. With Blake, Lawrence shares the conviction that touch, the sexual sense proper, is the least fallen of the senses, which implies that redemption is most readily a sexual process. Freud and Lawrence, according to Lawrence, share little or nothing, which accounts for Lawrence's ill-informed but wonderfully vigorous polemic against Freud:

> This is the moral dilemma of psychoanalysis. The analyst set out to cure neurotic humanity by removing the cause of the neurosis. He finds that the cause of neurosis lies in some unadmitted sex desire. After all he has said about inhibition of normal sex, he is brought at last to realize that at the root of almost every neurosis lies some incest-craving, and that this incest-craving is *not the result of inhibition and normal sex-craving*. Now see the dilemma—it is a fearful one. If the incest-craving is not the outcome of any inhibition of normal desire, if it actually exists and refuses to give way before any criticism, what then? What remains but to accept it as part of the normal sex-manifestation?
>
> Here is an issue which analysis is perfectly willing to face. Among themselves the analysts are bound to accept the incest-craving as part of the normal sexuality of man, normal, but suppressed, because of moral and perhaps biological fear. Once, however, you accept the incest-craving as

part of the normal sexuality of man, you must remove all repression of incest itself. In fact, you must admit incest as you now admit sexual marriage, as a duty even. Since at last it works out that neurosis is not the result of inhibition of so-called *normal* sex, but of inhibition of incest-craving. Any inhibition must be wrong, since inevitably in the end it causes neurosis and insanity. Therefore the inhibition of incest-craving is wrong, and this wrong is the cause of practically all modern neurosis and insanity.

To believe that Freud thought that "any inhibition must be wrong" is merely outrageous. Philip Rieff subtly defends Lawrence's weird accusation by remarking that: "As a concept, the incest taboo, like any other Freudian hypothesis, represents a scientific projection of the false standards governing erotic relations within the family." Lawrence surely sensed this, but chose to misunderstand Freud, for some of the same reasons he chose to misunderstand Walt Whitman. Whitman provoked in Lawrence an anxiety of influence in regard to stance and form. Freud, also too authentic a precursor, threatened Lawrence's therapeutic originality. Like Freud, Lawrence's ideas of drive or will stem from Schopenhauer and from Nietzsche, and again like Freud, Lawrence derived considerable stimulus from later nineteenth-century materialistic thought. It is difficult to remember that so flamboyant a mythmaker as Lawrence was also a deidealizer with a reductionist aspect, but then we do not see that Freud was a great mythmaker only because we tend to believe in Freud's myths. When I was young, I knew many young women and young men who believed in Lawrence's myths, but they all have weathered the belief, and I do not encounter any Lawrentian believers among the young today.

Rereading *The Rainbow* and *Women in Love* after many years, I find them very different from what I had remembered. Decades ago I knew both books so thoroughly that I could anticipate most paragraphs, let alone chapters, but I too had half-believed in Lawrence, and had read as a half-believer. Now the books seem richer and stranger, clearly an audacious and relevant myth, and far more original than I had recalled. States of being, modes of consciousness, ambivalences of the will are represented with a clarity and vividness that are uncanny, because the ease of representation for such difficult apprehensions seems unprecedented in prose fiction. Lawrence at his strongest is an astonishing writer, adept at saying what cannot be said, showing what cannot be shown. *The Rainbow* and, even more, *Women in Love* are his triumphs, matched only by a few of his poems, though by many of his short stories. In the endless war between men and women, Lawrence fights on both sides. He is unmatched at rendering really murderous lovers' quarrels, as in chapter 23, "Excurse," of *Women in Love*, where Ursula and Birkin suffer one of their encounters upon what Lawrence calls "this memorable battlefield":

> "I jealous! I—jealous! You *are* mistaken if you think that. I'm not jealous in the least of Hermione, she is nothing to me, not *that!*" And Ursula snapped her fingers. "No, it's you who are a liar. It's you who must return, like a dog to his vomit. It is what Hermione *stands* for that I *hate*. I hate it. It is lies, it is false, it is death. But you want it, you can't help it, you can't help yourself. You belong to that old, deathly way of living—then go back to it. But don't come to me, for I've nothing to do with it."
>
> And in the stress of her violent emotion, she got down from the car and went to the hedgerow, picking unconsciously some flesh-pink spindleberries, some of which were burst, showing their orange seeds.
>
> "Ah, you are a fool," he cried bitterly, with some contempt.
>
> "Yes, I am. I *am* a fool. And thank God for it. I'm too big a fool to swallow your cleverness. God be praised. You go to your women—go to them—they are your sort—you've always had a string of them trailing after you—and you always will. Go to your spiritual brides—but don't come to me as well, because I'm not having any, thank you. You're not satisfied, are you? Your spiritual brides can't give you what you want, they aren't common and fleshy enough for you, aren't they? So you come to me, and keep them in the background! You will marry me for daily use. But you'll keep yourself well provided with spiritual brides in the background. I know your dirty little game." Suddenly a flame ran over her, and she stamped her foot madly on the road, and he winced, afraid that she would strike him. "And, *I, I'm* not spiritual enough, *I'm* not as spiritual as that Hermione—!" Her brows knitted, her eyes blazed like a tiger's. "Then *go* to her, that's all I say, *go* to her, *go*. Ha, she spiritual—*spiritual*, she! A dirty materialist as she is. *She*

spiritual? What does she care for, what is her spirituality? What *is* it?" Her fury seemed to blaze out and burn his face. He shrank a little. "I tell you, it's *dirt, dirt,* and nothing *but* dirt. And it's dirt you want, you crave for it. Spiritual! Is *that* spiritual, her bullying, her conceit, her sordid, materialism? She's a fishwife, a fishwife, she is such a materialist. And all so sordid. What does she work out to, in the end, with all her social passion, as you call it. Social passion— what social passion has she?—show it me!—where is it? She wants petty, immediate *power,* she wants the illusion that she is a great woman, that is all. In her soul she's a devilish unbeliever, common as dirt. That's what she is, at the bottom. And all the rest is pretence—but you love it. You love the sham spirituality, it's your food. And why? Because of the dirt underneath. Do you think I don't know the foulness of your sex life—and hers?—I do. And it's that foulness you want, you liar. Then have it, have it. You're such a liar."

She turned away, spasmodically tearing the twigs of spindleberry from the hedge, and fastening them, with vibrating fingers, in the bosom of her coat.

He stood watching in silence. A wonderful tenderness burned in him at the sight of her quivering, so sensitive fingers: and at the same time he was full of rage and callousness.

This passage-at-arms moves between Ursula's unconscious picking of the fleshly, burst spindleberries, open to their seeds, and her turning away, tearing the spindleberry twigs so as to fasten them in her coat. Birkin reads the spindleberries as the exposed flesh of what Freud called one's own bodily ego, suffering here a *sparagmos* by a maenad-like Ursula. It is as though Birkin himself, lashed by her language, becomes a frontier being, caught between psyche and body. Repelled yet simultaneously drawn by a sort of Orphic wonder, Birkin yields to her ferocity that is not so much jealousy as it is the woman's protest against Birkin's Lawrentian and male idealization of sexual love. What Ursula most deeply rejects is that the idealization is both flawed and ambivalent, because it is founded upon a displaced Protestantism that both craves total union and cannot abide such annihilation of individuality. Birkin-Lawrence has in him the taint of the Protestant

God, and implicitly is always announcing to Ursula: "Be like me, but do not dare to be too like me!" an injunction that necessarily infuriates Ursula. Since Lawrence is both Birkin and Ursula, he has the curious trait, for a novelist, of perpetually infuriating himself.

II

Lawrence compares oddly with the other major British writers of fiction in this century: Hardy, Conrad, Kipling, Joyce, Forster, Woolf, Beckett. He is primarily a religious writer, precisely apocalyptic; they are not, unless you count Beckett, by negation. His last book, *Apocalypse*, written as he died slowly in the winter of 1929–30, begins with Lawrence remembering that his own first feeling about the Revelation of John, and indeed of the entire Bible, was negative:

Perhaps the most detestable of all these books of the Bible, taken superficially, is Revelation. By the time I was ten, I am sure I had heard, and read, that book ten times over, even without knowing or taking real heed. And without ever knowing or thinking about it, I am sure it always roused in me a real dislike. Without realising it, I must, from earliest childhood have detested the pie-pie, mouthing, solemn, portentous, loud way in which everybody read the Bible, whether it was parsons or teachers or ordinary persons. I dislike the "parson" voice through and through my bones. And this voice, I remember, was always at its worst when mouthing out some portion of Revelation. Even the phrases that still fascinate me I cannot recall without shuddering, because I can still hear the portentous declamation of a nonconformist clergyman: "And I saw heaven opened, and behold a white horse; and he that sat upon it was called"—there my memory suddenly stops, deliberately blotting out the next words: "Faithful and True." I hated, even as a child, allegory: people having the names of mere qualities, like this somebody on a white horse, called "Faithful and True." In the same way I could never read *Pilgrim's Progress*. When as a small boy I learnt from Euclid that: "The whole is greater than the part," I immediately knew that that solved the problem of allegory for me. A man is more than a Christian, a rider on a white horse must be more than mere

Faithfulness and Truth, and when people are mere personifi-
cations of qualities they cease to be people for me. Though
as a young man I almost loved Spenser and his *Faerie Queene*,
I had to gulp at his allegory.

Yet by the end of his book, Lawrence has allegorized Revelation
into "the dark side of Christianity, of individualism, and of democracy, the side the world at large now shows us." This side Lawrence
simply calls "suicide":

The Apocalypse shows us what we are resisting, unnaturally. We are unnaturally resisting our connection with the
cosmos, with the world, with mankind, with the nation,
with the family. All these connections are, in the Apocalypse, anathema, and they are anathema to us. We *cannot
bear connection*. That is our malady. We *must* break away, and
be isolate. We call that beign free, being individual. Beyond
a certain point, which we have reached, it is suicide. Perhaps
we have chosen suicide. Well and good. The Apocalypse too
chose suicide, with subsequent self-glorification.

This would seem to be no longer the voice of Birkin, who in
effect said to Ursula, "We *must* break away, and be isolate," but who
never learned how to stress properly his antithetical desire for connection. Lawrence, approaching his own end, is suddenly moved to what
may be his single most powerful utterance, surpassing even the greatest passages in the fiction and the late poetry:

But the Apocalypse shows, by its very resistance, the things
that the human heart secretly yearns after. By the very frenzy
with which the Apocalypse destroys the sun and the stars,
the world, and all kings and all rulers, all scarlet and purple
and cinnamon, all harlots, finally all men altogether who are
not "sealed," we can see how deeply the apocalyptists are
yearning for the sun and the stars and the earth and the
waters of the earth, for nobility and lordship and might, and
scarlet and gold splendour, for passionate love, and a proper
unison with men, apart from this sealing business. What
man most passionately wants is his living wholeness and his
living unison, not his own isolate salvation of his "soul."
Man wants his physical fulfillment first and foremost, since
now, once and once only, he is in the flesh and potent. For

man, the vast marvel is to be alive. For man, as for flower and beast and bird, the supreme triumph is to be most vividly, most perfectly alive. Whatever the unborn and the dead may know, they cannot know the beauty, the marvel of being alive in the flesh. The dead may look after the afterwards. But the magnificent here and now of life in the flesh is ours, and ours alone, and ours only for a time. We ought to dance with rapture that we should be alive and in the flesh, and part of the living, incarnate cosmos. I am part of the sun as my eye is part of me. That I am part of the earth my feet know perfectly, and my blood is part of the sea. My soul knows that I am part of the human race, my soul is an organic part of the great human soul, as my spirit is part of my nation. In my own very self, I am part of my family. There is nothing of me that is alone and absolute except my mind, and we shall find that the mind has no existence by itself, it is only the glitter of the sun on the surface of the waters.

Starting with the shrewd realization that apocalyptic frenzy is a reaction-formation to a deep yearning for fulfillment, this celebratory passage moves rapidly into an ecstasy of heroic vitalism, transcending the Zarathustra of Nietzsche and the related reveries of Pater in the "Conclusion" to *The Renaissance*. Lawrence may not have known that these were his ancestral texts in this rhapsody, but I suspect that he deliberately transumes Pater's "we have an interval, and then our place knows us no more," in his own: "But the magnificent here and now of life in the flesh is ours, and ours alone, and ours only for a time." Pater, hesitant and elaborate, skeptical and masochistic, added: "For our one chance lies in expanding that interval, in getting as many pulsations as possible into the given time." Lawrence, truly apocalyptic only in his vitalism, aligns himself rather with Whitman and Blake in refusing that aesthetic one chance, in favor of the dream of becoming integral, rather than a fragment:

What we want is to destroy our false, inorganic connections, especially those related to money, and re-establish the living organic connections, with the cosmos, the sun and earth, with mankind and nation and family. Start with the sun, and the rest will slowly, slowly happen.

Two in One: The Second Period

H. M. Daleski

Of the characters in *Women in Love* it is Birkin and Ursula who are most aware of the disintegration of life that the novel variously discloses. When he tells her that he is "tired of the life that belongs to death—our kind of life," he gives expression to her own intuitive sense of life as "a rotary motion, mechanized, cut off from reality. There was nothing to look for from life—it was the same in all countries and all peoples. The only window was death"; and it is their mutual recoil from a society *in extremis* that, in part, brings them together. Their relationship is the more momentous in that it is all they have to set against the general disaster, Birkin going so far as to say, in an early conversation with Gerald, that "there remains only this perfect union with a woman—sort of ultimate marriage—and there isn't anything else." It is not surprising that, rejecting the society he lives in, Birkin feels forced to seek a new kind of relation with Ursula, for it is clearly shown in the novel that the personal relations to which that society gives rise are themselves an alarming symptom of disease in the body politic.

The problem, as it presents itself in both its personal and social aspects, is primarily concerned with the difficulty of achieving a self, and this difficulty is seen to be at the centre of a particularly vicious circle. In the case of Gerald, for instance, it is because he loses all sense of an organic wholeness of being in his work in the mines that he has no independent self on which to lean in his fatal relationship with Gudrun; but it is only because he has no real self to start with, and no

From *The Forked Flame: A Study of D. H. Lawrence.* © 1965 by H. M. Daleski. Northwestern University Press, 1965.

respect for the claims of individuality, that he lends himself to the monstrous perversity which degrades the miners to mere instruments. It is the failure to consummate a self that undermines life, and in considering the sort of relationship he wishes to establish with Ursula, Birkin fastens on this deficiency in "the old way of love" as that which it is essential to avoid. Birkin meditates on this subject at length and with some obscurity, but in so far as his views are identifiable with those of Lawrence himself, as would seem likely, they are of central importance for an understanding of the development of Lawrence's thought:

> On the whole, he hated sex, it was such a limitation. It was sex that turned a man into a broken half of a couple, the woman into the other broken half. And he wanted to be single in himself, the woman single in herself. He wanted sex to revert to the level of the other appetites, to be regarded as a functional process, not as a fulfilment. He believed in sex marriage. But beyond this, he wanted a further conjunction, where man had being and woman had being, two pure beings, each constituting the freedom of the other, balancing each other like two poles of one force, like two angels, or two demons.
>
> He wanted so much to be free, not under the compulsion of any need for unification, or tortured by unsatisfied desire. Desire and aspiration should find their object without all this torture, as now, in a world of plenty of water, simple thirst is inconsiderable, satisfied almost unconsciously. And he wanted to be with Ursula as free as with himself, single and clear and cool, yet balanced, polarized with her. The merging, the clutching, the mingling of love was become madly abhorrent to him.
>
> But it seemed to him, woman was always so horrible and clutching, she had such a lust for possession, a greed of self-importance in love. She wanted to have, to own, to control, to be dominant. Everything must be referred back to her, to Woman, the Great Mother of everything, out of whom proceeded everything and to whom everything must finally be rendered up.
>
> It filled him with almost insane fury, this calm assumption of the Magna Mater, that all was hers, because she had

borne it. Man was hers because she had borne him. A Mater Dolorosa, she had borne him, a Magna Mater, she now claimed him again, soul and body, sex, meaning, and all. He had a horror of the Magna Mater, she was detestable. . . .

It was intolerable, this possession at the hands of woman. Always a man must be considered as the broken-off fragment of a woman, and the sex was the still aching scar of the laceration. Man must be added on to a woman, before he had any real place or wholeness.

And why? Why should we consider ourselves, men and women, as broken fragments of one whole? It is not true. We are not broken fragments of one whole. Rather we are the singling away into purity and clear being, of things that were mixed. Rather the sex is that which remains in us of the mixed, the unresolved. And passion is the further separating of this mixture, that which is manly being taken into the being of the man, that which is womanly passing to the woman, till the two are clear and whole as angels, the admixture of sex in the highest sense surpassed, leaving two single beings constellated together like two stars.

In the old age, before sex was, we were mixed, each one a mixture. The process of singling into individuality resulted into the great polarization of sex. The womanly drew to one side, the manly to the other. But the separation was imperfect even then. And so our world-cycle passes. There is now to come the new day, when we are beings each of us, fulfilled in difference. The man is pure man, the woman pure woman, they are perfectly polarized. But there is no longer any of the horrible merging, mingling self-abnegation of love. There is only the pure duality of polar-ization, each one free from any contamination of the other. In each, the individual is primal, sex is subordinate, but perfectly polarized. Each has a single, separate being, with its own laws. The man has his pure freedom, the woman hers. Each acknowledges the perfection of the polarized sex-circuit. Each admits the different nature in the other.

The repeated phrases in which man is described as "a broken half of a couple," "the broken-off fragment of a woman," and the "broken fragment of one whole" recall passages in *The Rainbow* in which Tom is said to be "the broken end of the arch" and in which Will realizes that "if [Anna] were taken away, he would collapse as a house from which the central pillar is removed." The phrases indicate, then, that Birkin is pursuing a line of thought which leads straight from the earlier novel; the quoted passage as a whole suggests that the line here curves in a new direction. The ideal relationship that Lawrence posits for the men and women of *The Rainbow* can be said to be the "two in one" that is symbolized by the rainbow arch; the relationship to which Birkin aspires with Ursula can best be described (in the terms in which Ursula thinks of it) as a "mutual unison in separateness," a phrase which registers a significant shift in emphasis. Though both phrases suggest a coming together in a union which does not obliterate single-ness, it seems to me that in the earlier phrase the emphasis is on union, whereas in the later it is on separateness. Birkin, certainly, is markedly preoccupied with the idea of "single, separate being." What, one wonders, is responsible for the change?

I suggest, in the first place, that the change reflects Lawrence's growing awareness of the extent to which individuality is threatened in the "man's world." In *The Rainbow*, Ursula declares that her life's task is to be the smashing of the machine; but the machine is so massively established in *Women in Love* that both she and Birkin abjure the fight and—as remains to be discussed—ultimately solve the difficulty by withdrawing from the world of work. The increasing menace of the machine is further indicated by the progression in the novels from Walter Morel, man and butty, to John Smith, loader, to Gerald's anonymous miner, instrument. It is as if man is now so squashed by the inexorable pressure of the outer world that the maintenance of individuality in his personal relations becomes of overriding impor-tance. For Birkin it is clearly of prime concern that what he refuses to yield to the machine should not be yielded to a woman, the more especially since he maintains that a "perfect union with a woman" is all that there is left to believe in. To yield to a woman, moreover, would likewise mean to submit to being exploited, to being reduced to an instrument.

Second, the change in emphasis is a measure of Lawrence's changed valuation of the significance of sexual intercourse. Hitherto the sex act has had a transcendent value in the sense that it has been regarded not merely as the means by which man and woman consummate their coming together but as the means by which they transcend their separateness in a union which is greater than either. In Lawrence's own terminology, indeed, the act may be said to have been viewed hitherto as a tangible manifestation of the Holy Ghost, the unifying Third Person of the Trinity. Birkin is the first character in Lawrence to think of sex "as a functional process, not as a fulfilment," and to regard the satisfaction of sexual desire as analogous to the satisfaction of thirst in a world of plenty of water. His "hatred" of "sex" is founded on the perception that it is destructive of the independence of man and woman, that, if it is once allowed a transcendent value, man and woman must of necessity be incomplete in themselves. In his insistent desire to be "single in himself" despite his conjunction with a woman, Birkin apparently wishes to fashion the house of marriage not round an arch but behind separate columns.

Birkin's demand that the individual be primal gains in force from our knowledge of Gerald's predicament, for Gerald's relationship with Gudrun, in one of its aspects, affords an instance of the "merging, mingling self-abnegation of love" which Birkin characterizes as "horrible." I suggest, however, that Birkin's demand should also be considered against the background of *The Rainbow*. It is not merely that Will's relations with Anna furnish us with an even better example of the attitudes Birkin castigates; in *The Rainbow* we can clearly see the limitations which attend the pursuit of "fulfilment" in a "sex marriage." Both Tom and Will do eventually find fulfilment in their marriages but only after an arduous struggle—and without succeeding in finding themselves. Neither, in the end, is "quite defined" as an individual. In *The Rainbow*, moreover, and it is this concept which seems to be especially pertinent to Birkin's meditations, the achievement of true individuality is regarded as being dependent on the reconciliation of male and female elements within the individual and on their maximum expression in a coherent personality; both Tom and Will, consequently, fail to attain to fullness of being because they manifestly exhaust their "man-being" in the sexual relation. It is a typical Lawrencean paradox that, as Birkin points out, and as Lawrence consistently asserts in his own person, the sex act is the means by which "the admixture of sex" is "surpassed," is the means, that is to say, by which the complex union of male and female components in the individual man and woman is reduced to elemental singleness, the man becoming "pure" man, the woman "pure" woman. The dilemma is formidable: "man-being" is exhausted in a consuming sexual relation; only the sex act is productive of an unadulterated "man-being." Birkin's reflections take a disconcerting turn when, in order to resolve the dilemma, he first minimizes the importance of the sex act and then predicates a "pure man" and "pure woman" who are "fulfilled in difference" not during sexual intercourse but, on the contrary, quite independently of such conjunction. Manhood and womanhood outside of the sexual relation are no longer, in other words, to be regarded as achievements, as the consummation of selves which have male and female components, but as singular blessings.

Birkin's conclusions are anticipatory of Lawrence's assertion in *Fantasia of the Unconscious* that "a child is either male or female, in the whole of its psyche and physique is either male or female." Whereas Lawrence takes his stand in the *Fantasia* statement, however, with unabashed dogmatism, it seems to me that in Birkin's meditations he resorts to obfuscation: we are first asked to accept the possibility of an "old age, before sex was" when we were "mixed"; then, while we are still bewildered by the curious phrase which qualifies the "old age," we are told of "the process of singling into individuality" which, even then, results in an imperfect separation between the manly and the womanly; finally, we are hastened on to the passing of "our world-cycle" and to the coming of "the new day" when man is "pure man" and woman "pure woman." In his depiction of the relations of Birkin and Ursula, I think we must assume, Lawrence tries to inaugurate the new day, and it is because he thereby drives himself into an untenable position that his treatment of their relationship, as I shall try to show, tends to be unsatisfactory. That it is an untenable position for him is sufficiently indicated in the quoted passage by the fact that, though a key concept governing the envisaged relation between man and woman is "the pure duality of polarization," when it comes to the individual, an arbitrary limit is set to the characteristic Lawrencean dualism. It is set, too, with such a violence of distaste—the "pure" man and woman are said to be "free from any contamination of the other"—as to be at once suspect. It is perhaps worth pointing out, in addition, that the images used to amplify the desiderated state of polarity are suggestive of a "non-human" relationship: the "two pure beings" balance each other "like two angels, or two demons" or they are "constellated together like two stars."

I have devoted so much attention to an analysis of Birkin's thoughts not only because they define the nature of the relationship he wishes to establish with Ursula, but also because they provide us with a key to an understanding of the symbolic action by which their relations are, in part, developed. There is a direct connection, for instance, between the passage I have quoted and the strange scene in which Birkin, unknowingly watched by Ursula, throws stone after stone at the reflection of the moon in the millpond. The scene itself is a central one, and it has links not only with other incidents in *Women in Love* but with *The Rainbow*. The effectiveness of the scene is increased if we realize that the moon has a symbolic value for Ursula as well as for Birkin, and that she in some measure intuitively comprehends the meaning of the stoning. The moon that is reflected in the pond is the moon that shone devastatingly on Skrebensky, the moon that is the planet of the self-assertive, sensual, devouring woman; and the chastening effect of Ursula's experiences with Skrebensky is suggested by her reaction when, on her way to the mill, she suddenly becomes aware of the moon: she "[suffers] from being exposed to it" and is glad "to pass into the shade," wishing for "something else out of the night . . . not this moon-brilliant hardness." She is "dazed" by Birkin's obsessive behaviour, feeling as if she has fallen and is "spilled out, like water on the earth," but in so far as she can understand what is occurring, she responds to his mood: after she has revealed herself they discuss their relationship, and she at once charges him with thinking that she only wants "physical things." The climax of the scene comes— and it is perhaps the best direct comment on one aspect of its complex symbolism—when Birkin's soft and gentle kisses none the less kindle "the old destructive fires" in Ursula: the fires, like the shattered moon which re-forms in the pond, are not easily extinguished, and though she at first submits to his plaintive request that they "be still," she cannot help cleaving close to him as he continues to kiss her. It is only by imposing "his idea and his will" that Birkin gets his way; rebuffed, Ursula puts on her hat and goes home.

I have said that the scene is also connected with Birkin's reflections on the "pure man" and "pure woman." His comments, in the quoted passage, on the possessive "Great Mother of everything" provide an obvious link with his stoning of the moon's reflection, for, putting a name to what Ursula vaguely but instinctively apprehends, he invokes Cybele, the "accursed Syria Dea," just before he begins to throw the stones. In a section (which I did not cite) from the same passage, Birkin indeed explicitly identifies both Ursula and Hermione with qualities of the Great Mother, "out of whom proceeded everything and to whom everything must finally be rendered up," thinking of Hermione as "the Mater Dolorosa, in her subservience, claiming with horrible, insidious arrogance and female tyranny, her own again," and of Ursula as "the same—or the inverse . . . the awful, arrogant queen of life" with "the unthinkable overweening assumption of primacy in her." We may add the name of Gudrun to the list, for, as we have seen, it is to a *magna mater* figure that Gerald does obeisance. While he is cursing Cybele, Birkin also throws the dead husks of flowers on to the water, apparently intimating, in a more restrained fashion than the frenzied stoning which follows, his determination to discard the forms of relationships that have gone dead.

Critical opinion evinces agreement, in general terms, on the immediate motivation of Birkin's unusual behaviour. It is only Eliseo Vivas who suggests a greater complexity of motivation. He finds the stoning revelatory of "the threat and the frustration that are tearing" Birkin:

> He curses Cybele, the Syria Dea, identified—or was it, confused?—in Greece with Aphrodite. She was a terrible goddess, for she destroyed the sacred king who mated with her on a mountain top by tearing out his sexual organs. She was served by sodomitic priests who dressed as women, castrated themselves, and sought ecstasy in union with her. I take it therefore that Birkin is expressing the ancient and deep-rooted fear some men have felt towards women.
>
> . . . Wanting Ursula, Birkin is also afraid that she will accept him, on any terms whatever. But it is not Ursula alone whom he has feared. He has feared Hermione and has broken with her for what he made to appear to be genuinely good reasons. Are we to gather that Birkin fears women and that at the root of his fear there is a component that he faces in the moon scene but does not dare face in its own literal terms, a component that taken together with his fear of woman leads us to the deep and sickly roots of the conflict between his need for love and his inability to accept or to give love?

This is an interesting interpretation, but I do not think it is supported by the facts of *Women in Love* as we have them. There is no indication I know of, other than the bare naming of Cybele, which by itself is hardly conclusive, that Birkin's relations with Ursula are undermined by the sort of fear Vivas suggests. The attribution of such a fear to Skrebensky, for instance, might be plausible, but the sexual relations of Birkin and Ursula, as described, are singularly free of the strain which attaches to Ursula's relations with Skrebensky in *The Rainbow*. Vivas stresses that the scene at the pond "takes place before the relationship between Birkin and Ursula becomes intimate," but this is simply not the case: the following passage from the earlier chapter, "Water-Party," is, I should say, quite unambiguous in that respect:

> And soon he was a perfect hard flame of passionate desire for her. Yet in the small core of the flame was an unyielding anguish of another thing. But this also was lost; he only wanted her, with an extreme desire that seemed inevitable as death, beyond question.
>
> Then, satisfied and shattered, fulfilled and destroyed, he went home away from her, drifting vaguely through the darkness, lapsed into the old fire of burning passion. Far away, far away, there seemed to be a small lament in the darkness. But what did it matter? What did it matter, what did anything matter save this ultimate and triumphant experience of physical passion, that had blazed up anew like a new spell of life. "I was becoming quite dead-alive, nothing but a word-bag," he said in triumph, scorning his other self. Yet somewhere far off and small, the other hovered.

This does not read like an experience which gives ground for the fear Vivas believes underlies the stone-throwing—Birkin feels "shattered" and "destroyed" only because he has been unable to resist what he conceives of as the destructive fire of passion, destructive in a way which I hope I have sufficiently discussed—nor is his supposed fear fed in any way by what follows. As for Hermione, it certainly seems a random speculation to suggest that Birkin's relations with her are vitiated by the same fear. Of that there is not the remotest indication, and Birkin does not have to make his reasons for breaking with her "appear to be genuinely good"; they are objectively established as such, and on quite other grounds. Birkin's cursing of Cybele, as I have tried to show, has a more general reference than that which Vivas attributes to it, though the castration rites associated with the goddess make her an appropriate symbol of all that Birkin fears is destructive of the male. When Vivas further contends—since Cybele's priests were not only "holy eunuchs" but also "sodomitic," that "another one of the frustrations" the scene at the pond expresses is related to the *Blutbrüderschaft* Birkin proposes to Gerald and to their naked wrestling, and hence to the possibility that Birkin is "projecting into [Ursula], or trying to find in her, what she [is] not and [cannot] be," I feel that, in regard to Birkin and Ursula, his attention should be drawn to his own stricture, in another connection, on "critics who inquire how many children Lady Macbeth had." As far as Birkin and Gerald are concerned, I shall try to show later that the significance of their wrestling is not that it points to a "theme of homosexuality," even if "we [use] the term ['homosexual'] in the broad sense we have learned from psychoanalysts," but that it helps to explain more clearly than "the myth of the *Vulva Dentata*" Birkin's "conflict between his need for love and his inability to accept or to give love."

There is, however, more to the stone-throwing than is at once apparent. A curious remark Birkin makes in reply to Ursula, when they are discussing his behaviour, alerts us to a further complexity of motivation on his part:

> "You won't throw any more stones, will you?"
> "I wanted to see if I could make it be quite gone off the pond," he said.
> "Yes, it was horrible, really. Why should you hate the moon? It hasn't done you any harm, has it?"
> "Was it hate?" he said.
> And they were silent for a few minutes.

When Birkin thinks of the *magna mater* in the passage which precedes the scene at the pond, he is so unambiguous and pronounced in his hatred of her—he has a "horror" of her, she is "detestable"—that we begin to wonder what else it is he sees in the reflected moon that gives rise to his ambivalent feeling. A clue to the additional meaning of the scene, I suggest, is to be found in the terms in which it is described: the smashing of the moon's reflection is persistently viewed in terms of a clash of opposites. The scene is set for us, so to speak, by Ursula, for we watch it through her eyes, and from the outset we are aware of the contrast between the brightness of the reflected moon and the darkness of the water: a fish leaps, "revealing the light in the pond," and "this fire of the chill night breaking constantly on to the pure darkness" repels her; she wishes it were "perfectly dark, perfectly, and noiseless and without motion." The image of the moon, we begin to understand, violates the purity of the dark waters, and it is the contaminating reflection that Birkin attempts to obliterate. The ambivalence of

Birkin's feeling towards the moon, after he has compulsively continued, "like a madness," to try to expunge it from the pond, may be attributed to the fact that the moon—quite apart from an esoteric mythology—is susceptible of a generalized identification with the feminine. The final "triumphant reassumption" of the reflected moon, which the dark waters cannot but contain, is in ironic opposition to Birkin's concept of the "pure man."

It strikes me as significant that the symbolic action which is used to develop the relationship of Birkin and Ursula should either, as in the case of the convincingly dramatic scene at the pond, be subversive of Birkin's pretensions both to eliminate the sensual *magna mater* in Ursula and to regard himself as a "pure" man, or, as in the case of the episode of the cats, to which I shall now refer, that it should be so palely ineffective, artistically. This incident, which is apparently intended to serve as an endorsement of the positive values which Birkin woos Ursula to acclaim in their relationship, can only be unfavourably compared with the brilliance of the scenes with the mare, the bullocks, or the rabbit, where the negative implications of Gerald and Gudrun's involvement with each other are subtly presented:

> "What I want is a strange conjunction with you—"[Birkin] said quietly; "—not meeting and mingling—you are quite right:—but an equilibrium, a pure balance of two single beings:—as the stars balance each other. . . ."
>
> "Isn't this rather sudden?" [Ursula] mocked.
>
> He began to laugh.
>
> "Best to read the terms of the contract, before we sign," he said.
>
> A young grey cat that had been sleeping on the sofa jumped down and stretched . . . Then it sat considering for a moment, erect and kingly. And then, like a dart, it had shot out of the room, through the open window-doors, and into the garden.
>
> "What's he after?" said Birkin, rising.
>
> The young cat trotted lordly down the path, waving his tail. He was an ordinary tabby with white paws, a slender young gentleman. A crouching, fluffy, brownish-grey cat was stealing up the side of the fence. The Mino walked statelily up to her, with manly nonchalance. She crouched before him and pressed herself on the ground in humility

. . . He looked casually down on her. So she crept a few inches further, proceeding on her way to the back door, crouching in a wonderful, soft, self-obliterating manner, and moving like a shadow.

He, going statelily on his slim legs, walked after her, then suddenly, for pure excess, he gave her a light cuff with his paw on the side of her face. She ran off a few steps, like a blown leaf along the ground, then crouched unobtrusively, in submissive, wild patience. . . .

"She is a wild cat," said Birkin. "She has come in from the woods. . . ."

"The wild cat," said Birkin, "doesn't mind. She perceives that it is justified."

"Does she!" cried Ursula. "And tell it to the Horse Marines."

"To them also."

"It is just like Gerald Crich with his horse—a lust for bullying—a real *Wille zur Macht*—so base, so petty."

"I agree that the *Wille zur Macht* is a base and petty thing. But with the Mino, it is the desire to bring this female cat into a pure stable equilibrium, a transcendent and abiding *rapport* with the single male. Whereas without him, as you see, she is a mere stray, a fluffy sporadic bit of chaos."

Ursula's reference to Gerald at once invites comparison between this scene and the episode at the railway crossing. It is obvious that, though the encounter of the cats is a pleasant enough interlude, and though it is an instance of Lawrence's gift for communicating his sense of the special quality, the "inwardness," of animal life, it is presented with nothing like the sustained power that characterizes the earlier description. It might be objected that power is hardly a fair criterion of comparison and that the account of the cats is deliberately modulated, but the power of Lawrence's writing is always a sure measure of the depth of his conviction; and if a lack of power is viewed here as a limitation, it is by way of suggesting that Lawrence has been unable to find an adequate symbolic equivalent for the idea of "a strange conjunction" to which Birkin alludes. Birkin's opening remarks, indeed, are a rather ostentatious prelude to what follows, and the crudity of the symbolic action in this case further sets it off from the incident at the crossing. The crudity betrays the employment of a clearly inferior technique: whereas Gerald and Gudrun are themselves participants in a self-contained and revelatory action which requires no overt comment as to its "meaning" on the part of the author, Birkin and Ursula are merely onlookers at the random meeting of the cats, which is introduced into the narrative in much the same way as the *exemplum* in a medieval sermon, with suitable embellishments both before and after and for similar purposes of edification. Finally, we ought not to be blind to the fact that the incident, as described, is itself inconsistent with Birkin's interpretation of its symbolism. An analysis of the encounter between the cats would seem to confirm Ursula's conclusion that what Birkin really wants is "a satellite," for Mino's behaviour is hardly illustrative, as he maintains, of a desire to bring the female cat into "a pure stable equilibrium, a transcendent and abiding *rapport* with the single male." The Mino's proudly single maleness is no doubt heavily asseverated—though "an ordinary tabby," he is "erect and kingly," he is "lordly," and he walks "statelily," with "manly nonchalance"—but whereas the supposed state of pure and stable equilibrium would seem to demand that he have a queenly consort, the sad truth is that the "wild cat" is very easily tamed. She starts off by "crouching" and by "stealing" up the fence; at the Mino's approach she presses herself on the ground "in humility" and creeps "a few inches" at a time; after the cuff she is duly "submissive." Perhaps the most revealing phrase, however, is that which refers to her "wonderful, soft, self-obliterating manner": the Mino remains unchallenged in his manly singleness, we see, because he has had the good fortune to encounter a self-less female, so utterly lacking in an independent being of her own, indeed, that she even moves "like a shadow." It begins regrettably but unavoidably to seem that Lawrence has demolished Cybele only to set up a new graven image in her stead—that of the triumphant male.

Pace Leavis, who says it seems to him that "the position for which Birkin contends in his wooing of Ursula does emerge from the 'tale' vindicated, in the sense that the norm he proposes for the relations of man and woman in marriage has been made, by the varied resources of Lawrence's art, sufficiently clear, and, in its intelligibility, sufficiently cogent, to compel us to a serious pondering," I must confess that I find the norm Birkin proposes, in so far as it is defined by the values he advocates rather than by those he rejects, neither clear nor cogent. I think that Lawrence's attempt to portray Birkin and Ursula's achievement of "the pure duality of polarization" (with all that the phrase, in its context, implies) is as unsatisfactory and unconvincing as the "doctrinal" passages in which he makes a frontal attack on our credence, and as the "symbolic" scenes in which he presents external support for his position. The means by which they achieve "polarity" are detailed in a crucial chapter called "Excurse"; the title, it seems, serves as an announcement, among other things, of a fresh sortie.

Some ten pages of "Excurse" are devoted to a description of the special kind of experience Birkin and Ursula have together and of its effect on them; I quote a representative passage, of manageable length:

> She looked at him. He seemed still so separate. New eyes were opened in her soul. She saw a strange creature from another world in him. It was as if she were enchanted, and everything were metamorphosed. She recalled again the old magic of the Book of Genesis, where the sons of God saw the daughters of men, that they were fair. And he was one of these, one of these strange creatures from the beyond, looking down at her, and seeing she was fair.
>
> He stood on the hearth-rug looking at her, at her face that was upturned exactly like a flower, a fresh, luminous flower, glinting faintly golden with the dew of the first light. And he was smiling faintly as if there were no speech in the world, save the silent delight of flowers in each other. Smilingly they delighted in each other's presence, pure presence, not to be thought of, even known. But his eyes had a faintly ironical contraction.
>
> And she was drawn to him strangely, as in a spell. Kneeling on the hearth-rug before him, she put her arms round his loins, and put her face against his thighs. Riches! Riches! She was overwhelmed with a sense of a heavenful of riches.
>
> "We love each other," she said in delight.
>
> "More than that," he answered, looking down at her with his glimmering, easy face.
>
> Unconsciously, with her sensitive finger-tips, she was tracing the back of his thighs, following some mysterious life-flow there. She had discovered something, something more than wonderful, more wonderful than life itself. It was the strange mystery of his life-motion, there, at the back of the thighs, down the flanks. It was a strange reality of his

being, the very stuff of being, there in the straight down-flow of the thighs. It was here she discovered him one of the sons of God such as were in the beginning of the world, not a man, something other, something more.

This was release at last. She had had lovers, she had known passion. But this was neither love nor passion. It was the daughters of men coming back to the sons of God, the strange inhuman sons of God, who are in the beginning.

Her face was now one dazzle of released, golden light, as she looked up at him and laid her hands full on his thighs, behind, as he stood before her. He looked down at her with a rich bright brow like a diadem above his eyes. She was beautiful as a new marvellous flower opened at his knees, a paradisal flower she was, beyond womanhood, such a flower of luminousness. Yet something was tight and unfree in him. He did not like this crouching, this radiance—not altogether.

It was all achieved for her. She had found one of the sons of God from the Beginning, and he had found one of the first most luminous daughters of men.

The ostensible meaning of this experience in the parlour of the inn is, I think, sufficiently clear—it is the means by which Birkin and Ursula establish their "unison in separateness"—but the experience, as described, is one in which, to say the least, it is difficult to participate imaginatively, and which leaves us both dissatisfied and puzzled. There is, for instance, the confusing issue of individual singleness. The delight they take in each other's presence, "pure presence," suggests that what we have here is the realization of the hopes that are set out in Birkin's reflections on the relations of men and women; but it is not clear whether the achieved "purity" is a product of the experience, or whether it is antecedent to it and merely ratified by what happens. On the one hand, even before Ursula touches Birkin, she sees him as one of "the sons of God": the reference to the mysterious passage in the Book of Genesis, it seems, does not only serve to assert Birkin's established independence of being but obscurely implies that his pure presence is also a matter of pure maleness, for the man who is "no son of Adam" can be assumed to be free from any contamination of the other sex. This, I take it, is what underlies the related assertions that he is "a strange creature from another world," and that he is "not a man" but "something other, something more." Similarly, Ursula is "beyond womanhood." If, then, the achievement of "pure individuality" is antecedent to the experience, we would like to know, for we are not told, just how it is that they are "metamorphosed."

On the other hand, it is later stated that their "accession into being" is directly due to the experience itself: "She seemed to faint beneath, and he seemed to faint, stooping over her. It was a perfect passing away for both of them, and at the same time the most intolerable accession into being." If the experience described were a phallic one, an accession into pure male and female being would be acceptably in line with typical Lawrencean thought, but the fact that it is not raises further difficulties. In the first place, though the nonphallic nature of the experience is stressed, it seems that we are intended to attribute to it the sort of transcendent value that is usually associated in Lawrence with the sex act: Ursula discovers "something more than wonderful, more wonderful than life itself," but what she discovers is "neither love nor passion." The "floods of ineffable darkness and ineffable riches," we are later told, that spring from "the smitten rock of the man's body, from the strange marvellous flanks and thighs," come from "deeper, further in mystery than the phallic source." I do not wish to suggest, of course, that the experience is represented as a substitute for sexual intercourse; on the contrary, once supreme value is attached to it and not to intercourse, sex, so to speak, is put safely in its place and ceases to be a menace. It is as if the experience is a means of controlling the "old destructive fires" which, as was earlier intimated in relation to Birkin's stoning of the moon's reflection, can never be entirely extinguished. Birkin and Ursula, indeed, after they have had tea at the inn, drive off into Sherwood Forest and, on a moonless night—"It was a night all darkness, with low cloud"— consummate their union in a more usual fashion. If what transpires in the forest, as the following quotation suggests, cannot be said to be analogous to the satisfaction of thirst in a world of plenty of water, its "perfection," I think, is intended to be viewed as a consequence of the revelation at the inn and its significance as subordinate to it:

> She had her desire of him, she touched, she received the
> maximum of unspeakable communication in touch, dark,
> subtle, positively silent, a magnificent gift and give again, a
> perfect acceptance and yielding, a mystery, the reality of
> that which can never be known, vital, sensual reality that

can never be transmuted into mind content, but remains outside, living body of darkness and silence and subtlety, the mystic body of reality. She had her desire fulfilled. He had his desire fulfilled. For she was to him what he was to her, the immemorial magnificence of mystic, palpable, real otherness.

If this analysis is acceptable, then it must further be urged that the experience at the inn is presented, rather too obviously, as an expedient by which the paradoxes inherent in Birkin's position are resolved; it is presented from one point of view, that is to say, as the means by which "pure" male and female being are attainable outside of sexual intercourse, and at the same time, in regard to the careful avoidance of any suggestion of "mingling and merging," or of any sense of containment, it is offered as a kind of sexual contact which, by its nature, cannot be either destructive or subversive of singleness. That it is an expedient is, in part, suggested by the poor quality of the writing. There is no call, I should say, for a detailed analysis of this weakness, for it is plainly evident in the passages I have cited, and there is general critical agreement, moreover, that the combined vagueness and stridency of the style hardly does Lawrence credit. The special pleading is also betrayed by the ridiculous lengths to which Lawrence is driven in attributing significance to the experience: after it, Ursula, who is said to be "usually nervous and uncertain at performing . . . public duties, such as giving tea," is "at her ease, entirely forgetting to have misgivings," and "the tea-pot [pours] beautifully from a proud slender spout"; similarly, when they are driving to Sherwood Forest, Birkin is described as sitting still "like an Egyptian Pharaoh, driving the car. He felt as if he were seated in immemorial potency, like the great carven statues of real Egypt, as real and as fulfilled with subtle strength, as these are, with a vague inscrutable smile on the lips," but lest there should be any doubt as to his ability to steer the vehicle, it is hastily asserted that the Egyptian in him is duly tempered by a touch of the Greek:

> But with a sort of second consciousness he steered the car towards a destination. For he had the free intelligence to direct his own ends. His arms and his breast and his head were rounded and living like those of the Greek, he had not the unawakened straight arms of the Egyptian, nor the sealed, slumbering head. A lambent intelligence played secondarily above his pure Egyptian concentration in darkness.

Even if we consider the description of the ultra-phallic revelation not so much as an expedient on Lawrence's part as a failure to communicate a genuine mystical experience, it seems open to serious objection. The failure in communication means that, at best, the experience remains the author's own, personal and not transmuted into the imaginative terms which alone could secure it a rightful place in a work of art; we are left, consequently, with little, if any, idea of what it is that actually happens to Birkin and Ursula at the inn. G. Wilson Knight attempts to relate the incident to the later account of anal intercourse in *Lady Chatterley's Lover*. He writes—I omit his parenthetical page references:

> Frontal, phallic, sexuality is surpassed, and an otherness touched "more wonderful than life itself"—a deathly otherness— "the very stuff of being" at "the darkest poles of the body" by the "rounded" loins, "the darkest, deepest, strangest life-source of the human body at the back and base of the loins". . . . In *Women in Love* the implements are fingers; but, as again in *Lady Chatterley*, it is a matter less of love than of deliberate and "impersonal" "sensual reality," and is to this extent "inhuman."
>
> ("Lawrence, Joyce and Powys")

Though I think we cannot be sure of the meaning of certain references in *Women in Love* if we attempt to explain them as they stand, there are passages which appear to be related to the description of "the shameful natural and unnatural acts of sensual voluptuousness" of Will and Anna in *The Rainbow*, and which, when read in the light of *Lady Chatterley's Lover*, would seem to confirm Wilson Knight's argument. Before Birkin and Ursula go to the inn, for instance, he thinks of how "he [has] taken her at the roots of her darkness and shame like a demon"; and later, Ursula is glad to realize "they might do as they liked. . . . How could anything that gave one satisfaction be excluded? What was degrading?" Nevertheless, I do not believe that the incident at the inn should be interpreted in this way. It is not merely that it is difficult to reconcile Wilson Knight's interpretation with the description, as we have it, of what transpires in the public parlour of the inn; after Birkin and Ursula leave the inn, we are told that he is still waiting "for her to take this knowledge of him as he [has] taken it of her." Nor, as I have already pointed out, does it seem to me that the description of the intercourse which follows suggests anything unconventional.

The failure in communication, then, would seem to preclude the relationship which Birkin ostensibly succeeds in establishing with Ursula from being regarded as in any sense normative, the norm which he proposes being, in the crucial instance of their sexual relations, if in no other, neither exoteric nor intelligible. Moreover, even if we assume, for the moment, that the description of the experience at the inn succeeds in suggesting the means by which a "pure stable equilibrium" between the lovers is to be assured, we cannot help noticing that the state of balance supposedly attained is precarious, if not equivocal. The scene, as Ursula kneels before Birkin, is a little too reminiscent of the wild cat and the Mino to be quite comfortable, and though it is said that Birkin does "not like this crouching, this radiance—not altogether," the disavowal, in its half-heartedness, is a disquieting intimation of what we are to expect in the next phase of Lawrence's writing, the phase which culminates in the blatant one-sidedness of the main relationships in *The Plumed Serpent*.

Ostensibly secure in their singleness, Birkin and Ursula are now ready for marriage, ready, that is, to be "transcended into a new oneness," to consummate their separate being in "a new, paradisal unit regained from the duality." The kind of marriage they wish to make, however, is more expressive of revolt against the established order, against "the horrible privacy of domestic and connubial satisfaction" and "the hot narrow intimacy between man and wife," than is the liaison of Gerald and Gudrun, and it implies no surrender to the society they despise. Indeed, it is over tea at the inn, immediately after the climactic revelation, that Birkin declares they must "drop [their] jobs," that "there's nothing for it but to get out, quick"; and it is "when they [wake] again from the pure swoon" which ensues on Ursula's "[pressing] her hands . . . down upon the source of darkness in him," that they decide "to write their resignations from the world of work there and then." Even fighting the old, as Ursula later tells Gudrun, means belonging to it, and their rejection of the world they know is absolute. It extends to a renunciation of all possessions, for Birkin maintains that "houses and furniture and clothes" are "all terms of an old base world, a detestable society of man," and in their determination to avoid having things of their own, they refuse to be bound even by a chair they had bought at a jumble market and give it away. Just what they will do and where they will go is not precisely defined. Birkin, who is fortunately possessed of a private income, suggests that they should "wander away from the world's somewheres into [their] own nowhere," contending that it is possible "to be free, in a free place, with a few other people," though he admits that it is not so much "a locality" he is seeking as "a perfected relation between [them], and others." In the event, they embark, together with Gerald and Gudrun, on the Alpine holiday. Though their decision to leave the mountain resort should be viewed, in contrast to the enthusiasm which Gerald and Gudrun evince for the cold whiteness, as indicative of the bid they are making for life, Gerald's death nevertheless forces them to return. It is with his death, so ominous in its implications for the "world" from which they are fleeing, that ultimately they are faced.

I have stressed Birkin and Ursula's desire to withdraw from the world because, in so far as Lawrence's feelings in this respect can be identified with theirs, their attitude represents a significant reversal of the attempt, begun in *The Rainbow*, to come to terms with it. In the earlier novel, it will be remembered, the realization of "man-being" was seen to be dependent on effective "utterance" in the "man's world," and Tom and Will and Skrebensky were, in different measure, condemned for a failure in manhood; it was only Ursula who could be said to have achieved full individuality. At the opening of *Women in Love* the prior struggles for integrated being of *The Rainbow* are, so to speak, taken for granted, in the sense that none of the four leading characters is subject to the limitations of "blood-intimacy": they are articulate, self-conscious, and intellectual; and all are active in the "world of work." The problem Lawrence apparently set himself was that of exploring the development of individuality with ever more and more complex characters, of proceeding, as it were, to a Birkin and an Ursula and a Gerald and a Gudrun through a Tom and a Lydia and a Will and an Anna. In *Women in Love* it becomes evident, however, that true being is more than a matter of having a day, as well as a night, goal. In the end, as I have previously pointed out, Gerald's work in the mines and Gudrun's art are revealed as "disintegrative," as an abuse of organic life; and the black sensuality of their relationship is productive of the violence which, in the novel, is seen as an inevitable concomitant of any process of "dissolution." What, then, of Birkin and Ursula? What are we to make of the fact that their "accession into being" is followed at once by their resignations from the "world of work?" Whether or not we are inclined to accept their ostensible achievement of genuine individuality, their withdrawal from the world—though it may perhaps be justified by the hopeless state of the society in which they would have to live if they did not withdraw from it—must be deemed, in the context of the two books, a serious qualification of their fullness of being. Accordingly, it should come as no surprise that, in the next phase of his writing, Lawrence should assiduously seek to determine the conditions under which a return to the world is possible, and that, given the collapse of the prewar world of *The Rainbow* and of *Women in Love*, such a return should ultimately necessitate the emergence of a leader who will try to refashion it.

With the crucial Hardy essay in mind, we may also view the arduous movement to the world and away from it and then back again as having a different, though of course related, motive force. Unlike the main male protagonists in *The Rainbow*, who strive to reconcile their male and female elements but who fail to do so, and who are on the whole dominated by tendencies which, in the essay, are said to exemplify the female principle, Birkin, a most Lawrence-like figure, is presented as believing in an unadulterated masculinity. The distinguishing quality of his manhood, however, his insistence on the primacy of being, turns out (again in terms of the essay) to be disconcertingly feminine in character. This insistence manifests itself as the most pronounced feature of his relationship with Ursula: separateness of being is a prime condition of their unison, and it is because the maintenance of individual being is paramount that he urges her to withdraw with him from the world. "Doing," "Public Good," and "Community" are typical attributes of the male principle as opposed to female "Being" and "Self-Establishment." It is therefore on essentially female terms, though in the name of a clear and determined manhood, that Birkin is set to live his life with Ursula. Again, it should not be found surprising that, in the next phase, there ultimately evolves the stern and relentless male who, in his personal relations with a woman, is an assertive and dominating figure, and who plays his part in the world as a leader of men.

Male elements in Birkin, which I think we must now view as existing in a state of insidious war with female elements rather than in a condition of triumphant and uncontaminated assumption, are manifested in his relationship with Gerald. He tells Gerald that he believes in "the *additional* perfect relationship between man and man—additional to marriage," and that this relationship should be "equally important, equally creative, equally sacred, if you like." His desire for such a relationship may be regarded as expressive of his revolt against the conventional relations of men and women, of defiance of the "whole community of mistrustful couples insulated in private houses or private rooms, always in couples, and no further life, no further immediate, no disinterested relationship admitted"; but it also suggests, as I shall now try to show, that he is urged to satisfy longings which, in relation to a woman, he feels compelled to resist. This is indicated when he proposes to Gerald that they should swear a *Blutbrüderschaft*. He makes the proposal when he realizes that he must face "the problem of love and eternal conjunction between two men," and when he first admits to himself that "to love a man purely and fully" has been "a necessity inside himself all his life."

> "You know how the old German knights used to swear a *Blutbrüderschaft*," he said to Gerald, with quite a new happy activity in his eyes.
> "Make a little wound in their arms, and rub each other's blood into the cut?" said Gerald.
> "Yes—and swear to be true to each other, of one blood, all their lives. That is what we ought to do. No wounds, that is obsolete. But we ought to swear to love each other, you and I, implicitly, and perfectly, finally, without any possibility of going back on it."
> He looked at Gerald with clear, happy eyes of discovery. Gerald looked down at him, attracted, so deeply bondaged in fascinated attraction, that he was mistrustful, resenting the bondage, hating the attraction.
> "We will swear to each other, one day, shall we?" pleaded Birkin. "We will swear to stand by each other—be true to each other—ultimately—infallibly—given to each other, organically—without possibility of taking back."

Birkin later adds, as Gerald shows less and less inclination to accept the offer, that what he wants is "an impersonal union that leaves one free," but it is noticeable that he actually lays more stress on unison than on separateness: they, like the German knights, should be "of one blood"; they should be "given to each other, organically." Moreover, though Birkin strenuously opposes (albeit not always successfully) Ursula's efforts to make him declare his love for her, since the word is tainted in his mind with connotations of "mingling and merging," he proposes a swearing of love as the oath of brotherhood. In other words, the typically "male" desire for a "melting into pure communion," for a "fusing together into oneness," is allowed expression only in relation to a man; for in such a relation, it seems, there is no defensive compulsion, as there is in regard to a woman, to realize the "otherness" of the partner.

I suggest that strong confirmation of this interpretation is to be found in the description of the well-known wrestling bout between Gerald and Birkin, which functions as a non-bloody, if not altogether acknowledged, pledge of brotherhood. The two men strip naked and begin "a real struggle," driving "deeper and deeper against each other, as if they would break into a oneness."

> So the two men entwined and wrestled with each other, working nearer and nearer. . . . [Birkin] seemed to penetrate into Gerald's more solid, more diffuse bulk, to interfuse his body through the body of the other, as if to bring it subtly into subjection, always seizing with some rapid necromantic foreknowledge every motion of the other flesh, converting and counteracting it, playing upon the limbs and trunk of Gerald like some hard wind. It was as if Birkin's whole physical intelligence interpenetrated into Gerald's body, as if his fine, sublimated energy entered into the flesh of the fuller man, like some potency, casting a fine net, a prison, through the muscles into the very depths of Gerald's physical being.
>
> So they wrestled swiftly, rapturously, intent and mindless at last, two essential white figures working into a tighter, closer oneness of struggle, with a strange, octopus-like knotting and flashing of limbs in the subdued light of the room; a tense white knot of flesh gripped in silence between the walls of old brown books. Now and again came a sharp gasp of breath, or a sound like a sigh, then the rapid thudding of movement on the thickly-carpeted floor, then the strange sound of flesh escaping under flesh. Often, in the white interlaced knot of violent living being that swayed silently, there was no head to be seen, only the swift, tight limbs, the solid white backs, the physical junction of two bodies clinched into oneness. Then would appear the gleaming, ruffled head of Gerald, as the struggle changed, then for a moment the dun-coloured, shadowlike head of the other man would lift up from the conflict, the eyes wide and dreadful and sightless.
>
> At length Gerald lay back inert on the carpet.

We can be reasonably confident, I think, that Lawrence did not intend this description to be overtly homosexual in character, though there is not much evidence of what he thought about homosexual practices. Cecil Gray, who is for the most part hostile to Lawrence, reports that in 1916 he read the typescript of an unpublished work called *Goats and Compasses*, which he describes as "a bombastic, pseudo-mystical, psycho-philosophical treatise dealing largely with homosexuality"; but since the only two copies of the "treatise" were destroyed, one by Lawrence himself and the other by Philip Heseltine, Gray's description of it testifies to nothing more than that Lawrence was interested in the subject—though Gray found his interest "suspiciously lively" (*Peter Warlock*). In *The Rainbow*, however, Lawrence is clearly critical of the "perverted life" of Winifred; and in his essay on Whitman he unequivocally states: "For the great mergers, woman at last becomes inadequate. . . . So the next step is the merging of man-for-man love. And this is on the brink of death. It slides over into death." Moreover, Catherine Carswell, who knew Lawrence well, records his detestation of sexual "perversion," and Knud Merrild, who lived for some time with him in New Mexico, insists on his undoubted "normality." It would seem, therefore, that the distinct homosexual colouring of the description of the wrestling bout—and of other scenes (such as the bathing scene in *The White Peacock*, the sick-room scene in *Aaron's Rod*, the scenes in which there are physical encounters between Somers and Kangaroo in *Kangaroo*, and the initiation scene in *The Plumed Serpent*) in which Lawrence portrays a close physical intimacy between men with one of whom he is more or less identified—is evidence of the pronounced feminine component in his make-up, of a latent or repressed homosexual tendency, rather than of any overt homosexual intention on his part.

The emotional force of the quoted description, however, suggests that the bout is meant to have an extraphysical significance, and indeed we are told that the wrestling has "some deep meaning to them—an unfinished meaning." It seems to me that we should regard it as parallel in function to the means by which Birkin and Ursula establish contact at the inn, though in the case of the man and the woman, of course, the occasion marks their full acceptance of the bond between them; whereas here the pledge to brotherhood—Birkin's reply to Gerald's question as to whether this is the *Brüderschaft* he wants being a noncommittal "Perhaps"—is only tentatively affirmed. If there is a parallelism between the scenes, then the differences between them are striking. First, the description of the wrestling is not marred by any of the mystical fogginess which clings to the account of what happens at the inn. Second, whereas the contact between man and woman preserves their separateness, that between man and man knots them together. It might be argued that "knotting" is an inescapable consequence of wrestling, but the references to their "oneness," as they wrestle "rapturously," are too insistent and (in the context of the book as a whole) too charged with meaning to be limited in their application to the merely physical facts of the tussle: they seem to drive deeper against each other, "as if they would break into a oneness"; as they "entwine," Birkin seems "to interfuse his body through the body of the other"; Birkin's "sublimated energy" casts "a fine net, a prison, through the muscles into the very depths of Gerald's physical being"; they work into a "tighter, closer oneness of struggle" as they become a "white interlaced knot of violent living being"; and, finally, there is to be seen only "the physical junction of two bodies clinched into oneness."

It is scarcely surprising that this pledge of brotherhood should come to nothing, for Birkin and Gerald obviously stand for radically different ways of life—virtually, indeed, for life as opposed to death. Nevertheless, at the end of the novel, Birkin is left to regret the fact that Gerald's death has put an effective end to his hopes of union with a man:

> "Did you need Gerald?" [Ursula] asked one evening.
> "Yes," he said.
> "Aren't I enough for you?" she asked.
> "No," he said. "You are enough for me, as far as a woman is concerned. You are all women to me. But I wanted a man friend, as eternal as you and I are eternal."
> "Why aren't I enough?" she said. "You are enough for me. I don't want anybody else but you. Why isn't it the same with you?"
> "Having you, I can live all my life without anybody else, any other sheer intimacy. But to make it complete, really happy, I wanted eternal union with a man too: another kind of love," he said.
> "I don't believe it," she said. "It's an obstinacy, a theory, a perversity."
> "Well " he said
> "You can't have two kinds of love. Why should you!"

"It seems as if I can't," he said. "Yet I wanted it."

"You can't have it, because it's false, impossible," she said.

"I don't believe that," he answered.

The "two kinds of love" which Birkin says he wanted should not be distinguished simply as love for a woman and love for a man: what is involved, as I have tried to show, is a need on his part both for firm singleness and for melting union. That Lawrence believes it is possible to reconcile these needs is suggested by the closing words of the novel, which, in their inconclusiveness, are anticipatory of the further consideration this problem is given in the next phase of his work. After the rigorous trial of *The Rainbow* and *Women in Love* he has, at last, in his portrayal of the relationship of Birkin and Ursula, ostensibly established the conditions of fruitful marriage; in *Aaron's Rod* we are, so to speak, invited to support Birkin's contention that a married man's desire for "eternal union with a man too" is not an obstinacy, nor a theory, nor a perversity.

The Revelation of the Unconscious

Peter K. Garrett

Women in Love [is] at once Lawrence's most schematic and his most symbolic novel. The novel's most extensive scheme elaborates its negative theme, the various paths of dissolution taken by both the individual and by the entire society, ranging between the extremes of the "African" and "Nordic" ways. It is the more exotic, African cluster of ideas and images which first clearly presents the theme of cultural dissolution in the pursuit of one extreme form of knowledge and being. Its emblems are the primitive sculptures in Halliday's rooms. One of these, a statue of a woman in labor, figures prominently in chapter 7, "Totem," where Birkin declares it to be art because it "contains the whole truth" of the state it expresses, the product of "an awful pitch of culture . . . pure culture in sensation, culture in the physical consciousness, really ultimate *physical* consciousness, mindless, utterly sensual." The significance of such a development in cultural history is pursued further in one of Birkin's meditations as he recalls another of the statues, West African, which represents an abandonment of all efforts at "pure integral being," turning to extreme refinements of sensual knowledge, "mystic knowledge in disintegration and dissolution." Birkin then realizes that there is another possible way which travels to the opposite extreme from "the long, long African process of purely sensual understanding, knowledge in the mystery of dissolution." "It would be done differently by the white races. The white races, having the Arctic north behind them, the vast

---

From *Scene and Symbol from George Eliot to James Joyce: Studies in Changing Fictional Mode.* © 1969 by Yale University. Yale University Press, 1969.

abstraction of ice and snow, would fulfill a mystery of ice-destructive knowledge, snow-abstract annihilation."

Gerald Crich is the chief representative of this northern mode of disintegration, and from his first appearance he is presented in arctic imagery: "In his clear northern flesh and his fair hair was a glisten like sunshine refracted through crystals of ice." When Birkin first conceives of the northern mode of dissolution he at once thinks of Gerald: "He was one of these strange white wonderful demons from the north, fulfilled in the destructive frost mystery. And was he fated to pass away in this knowledge, this one process of frost-knowledge, death by perfect cold? Was he a messenger, an omen of the universal dissolution into whiteness and snow?" The metaphors become literalized in the novel's concluding section, where, under Gerald's leadership, the central quartet of characters moves into the frozen white Alpine world. Here, in an inversion of pathetic fallacy, the symbolic landscape seems to project its meaning on the characters' minds: "The first days passed in an ecstasy of physical motion, sleighing, ski-ing, skating, moving in an intensity of speed and white light that surpassed life itself, and carried the souls of the human beings beyond into an inhuman abstraction of velocity and weight and eternal, frozen snow." Birkin and Ursula, committed to "the old effort at serious living," unwilling to "fall from the connection with life and hope," to cease the attempt at "pure integral being," turn from this landscape of Nordic dissolution to the warm lands of the south, leaving the others to their chosen fates—Gerald's actual "death by perfect cold," and Gudrun's further pursuit of "ultimate reduction . . . disintegrating the vital organic body of life."

I have sketched only the most prominent elements of this thematic pattern, whose pervasive ramifications include numerous other images and characters, scenes and statements. Water and mud and the water plants which grow out of them, the "flowers of dissolution—fleurs du mal" with which Gudrun and Gerald are associated become part of the pattern, as do machines and industry, and debates about the role of the will. Lawrence's pattern underlies his schematic presentation of society; the country house world of Breadalby or the bohemian one of the Pompadour Café, that "small, slow central whirlpool of disintegration and dissolution," are two of the more carefully exhibited specimens of the process at work in the entire society, just as Hermione, hysterical advocate of the will, and Loerke, the artist in the service of the machine, "the wizard rat" swimming ahead in "the river of corruption," provide further individual variants. All these elements and many more are controlled by the fundamental scheme which locates each instance of dissolution within the spectrum which extends from the African to the Nordic extreme.

Imagery alone might suffice to embody the theme of dissolution, but not to make the analytical discriminations between its various modes which Lawrence's scheme requires. Such discriminations are essentially conceptual, and to establish them Lawrence must introduce the concepts on which they are based, hence the large role played in the novel by debates between the characters, by individuals' meditations, and by the commentary and analysis of Lawrence's narrator. Here conceptual terms and ideas are introduced which provide a firm context for individual scenes. As we have seen in the case of George Eliot, such a well-established conceptual context creates a strong field of attraction, along whose lines of force images, characters, and events may be drawn. The effect is carried much further in *Women in Love*, creating a more pervasive symbolic quality, a greater potential for thematic significance in each detail than we have found in any of the novels previously examined. This aspect of Lawrence's symbolism is perfectly consonant with his schematism, and it is therefore the aspect with the strongest tendency toward allegory, toward placing action, image, and character entirely in the service of conceptual theme. We can see the predominance of such allegorization in Lawrence's presentation of Gerald as industrial magnate, which as [Eliseo] Vivas notes is developed in "essentially . . . conceptual" terms, but we also find such schematism complicated in the presentation of Gerald as Birkin's friend or Gudrun's lover (*D. H. Lawrence*). Yet, as I have already indicated, I believe that this sort of complexity is not the most important nonschematic factor in Lawrence's fictional mode, that this factor is to be found instead in certain of his symbolic scenes.

Some scenes of *Women in Love* owe their symbolic quality almost entirely to their place in its thematic patterns. An example is the brief scene at the beginning of chapter 4 where Ursula and Gudrun watch Gerald swimming and Gudrun envies the masculine freedom his act represents. The chapter's title, "Diver," creates a significant emphasis, suggesting a meaningfulness in presenting Gerald in terms of this action, but our understanding of this meaning must be retrospective, taking his action in the context of subsequent events and thematic patterns. Gerald appears again as a diver in "Breadalby" and "Waterparty," but the symbolic relevance does not emerge until much later, although in the latter scene, after futilely diving after his drowned sister, he utters reflections which hint at the doom which is coming not only for himself but for an entire civilization. "There's room under that water there for thousands . . . a whole universe under there; and as cold as hell, you're as helpless as if your head was cut off." The significance of these words, however, is also dependent on contextual terms which have yet to be introduced, Birkin's conception of the northern fate. In the end, as helpless as if beheaded because his cardinal principles of mind and will have failed, Gerald takes his last dive, into the hollow basin of snow, where he meets his death by perfect cold. In the light of the novel's entire pattern, the earlier diving scenes become symbolic. In the first, despite the chapter's title, Gerald appears as swimmer more than as diver, and on the surface of the water he is magnificently capable, as much so as in his role of industrial magnate. But in retrospect we recognize the aptness of Lawrence's title: the impulse which will prevail is that toward the icy depths, the "quick jump downwards, in a sort of ecstasy," contrasted to Gudrun's prolonged exploration of the "myriad subtle thrills of reduction," both part of the northern mode of dissolution.

There are other symbolic scenes which seem to be just as fully in the service of the novel's thematic context yet whose significance is not so completely dependent on it. A striking example is the scene in which Gerald forces his horse to stand at the railroad crossing while a train passes. Vivas calls the scene a "quasi-symbol" because "its meaning is given us discursively in Chapter XII, 'Carpeting' and in XVII, 'The Industrial Magnate.' " In the first of these two chapters, Gerald defends his brutal subjugation of the mare as necessary to make her useful to him. The other, of course, contains Lawrence's main exposition of Gerald as "the God of the machine," who has "conceived the pure instrumentality of mankind." Here the general cultural significance of his industrial ethic is clearly expounded:

> It was the first great step in undoing, the first great phase of chaos, the substitution of the mechanical principle for the organic, the destruction of the organic purpose, the organic unity, and the subordination of every organic unit to the great mechanical purpose. It was pure organic disintegration and pure mechanical organization. This is the first and finest stage of chaos.

As Vivas's statement implies, we might read the earlier scene as a simple allegorization of these concepts: in subduing the terrified horse

Gerald demonstrates his will to dominate and clearly subordinates the organic, the fine, sensitive Arab mare, to the mechanical, the rumbling coal train. Yet this meaning is clear in the scene; unlike the diver scenes, it is not dependent on the later passages, which reexpress its significance discursively, generalize it, and relate it to the novel's thematic patterns.

The scene is symbolic in that it concentrates this general significance in a concrete, dramatic action, but it also derives a symbolic quality, not dependent on later thematic statements, from the great intensity it develops in itself. The terror of the horse and the cold violence with which Gerald asserts his will, their powerful effect on Ursula, and especially on Gudrun, whose underlying sadistic and masochistic nature responds to their impact—the way in which the scene is indeed made almost as great an ordeal for the reader—all contribute to its intensity, an intensity which has the effect of insisting on its significance, on the depth of the psychic states in Gerald and Gudrun which it partially reveals. Thus it would be wrong to suggest that the scene creates only a thin allegorical veneer over conceptual meanings. Even though its central explicable meaning is presented elsewhere, there is no split between the scene and its meaning. Its intensity furthermore confers a degree of independence on it which suggests the way in which other symbolic scenes may have a still more complicated relation to their context. It is, after all, not too great a step from this scene to that of Gudrun, Gerald, and the rabbit, which Vivas calls a constitutive symbol. The absolute opposition of "pseudo-symbol" and "constitutive symbol" is easier to maintain in theory than in the close examination of artistic practice.

As the last car in the train passes, Gudrun imagines how the scene in which she has participated must look to the guard within, appearing "spectacularly, isolated, and momentary, like a vision isolated in eternity." Many of the novel's scenes have such a spectacular quality and stand in formal isolation because of the narrative's discontinuity. They thus acquire a degree of significance, a portentous quality, even when their specific symbolic significance is not apparent, and when it is, as in the scene we have just considered, the emphasis created by their spectacular isolation increases its intensity. The narrative discontinuity of *Women in Love* is characteristic of the modern, symbolic mode. The arrangement of material is controlled by a structure of significance, replacing the traditional plot with its structure of causally related events. The formal isolation of components allows their significance to emerge more clearly; the pattern of meaning, of parallels or contrasts between scenes, is not obscured by the pattern of a plot which also relates them on another level. We can see the beginnings of such discontinuity in James's later novels, such as *The Wings of the Dove*, which contains several sharp breaks in the narrative and whose significant omission of certain crucial scenes is part of a general symbolic method. Conrad's fiction tends more clearly toward such an effect. His disruption of a linear temporal progression weakens the causal relations between events, allowing for significant rearrangement. In Joyce we shall find the fullest fictional development of symbolic structural principles, and the tendency is even more obvious in the contemporary poetry which takes extended forms. *The Waste Land* or Pound's *Cantos* provide outstanding examples of formal discontinuity and symbolic form. In the development of a symbolic mode, fiction moves in the direction of poetry.

But the nature of fiction always requires a higher degree of continuity than does comparably motivated poetry. Auden, in noting Lawrence's concern with states rather than individuals, also indicates the problems such motivation creates for the writer of narrative: "In writing about nature or strangers this does not matter, as these are only experienced as states of being, but it is a serious drawback in writing fiction which cannot avoid the individual and his relations to other individuals over a stretch of time" ("Some Notes on D. H. Lawrence"). In *The Rainbow* and *Women in Love* Lawrence tends to disregard much of the realistic, social level of his characters' relation to each other, attempting to reveal their relations on a deeper level, where they exist as elemental states. Scenes which reveal these states of being in isolated, spectacular moments are related by a pattern of thematic concepts *about* such states. As David Gordon observes, Lawrence thus solves his narrative problem "by submitting his material to a kind of allegorical scheme by means of which the parts relate to one another not so much causally or consecutively as analogically" (*D. H. Lawrence as a Literary Critic*). It is a strategy of poetry, even, as Mr. Gordon notes, of allegorical poetry: "roughly comparable to that in *The Faerie Queene*."

The most intense and profound of Lawrence's symbolic scenes, however, seem to exceed the requirements of his allegorical scheme and thus to develop a kind of resistance to its gravitational attraction. One of the most successful of such scenes is the one which provides the title for chapter 18, "Rabbit." Elements of its meaning both draw on and reinforce the novel's established themes. Again we see in

Gerald the assertion of will, the subordination of the organic and vital, again symbolized in the subjection of an animal, in which Gudrun this time also participates. In this respect, the scene might appear even more fully controlled by Lawrence's conceptual presentation of Gerald than the one with the horse, since it follows immediately after the "Industrial Magnate" chapter. But here Lawrence places his central emphasis on the revelation of psychic states which are only presented peripherally in the earlier scene. The intensity of these states and Lawrence's ability to present them convincingly as deep, hidden, secret recesses within the characters establishes the scene's meaning on a different level.

The scene is mysterious, like the rabbit itself: " 'Bismarck is a mystery, Bismarck, c'est un mystère, der Bismarck, er ist ein Wunder,' said Gudrun in mocking incantation," establishing the tone at the scene's beginning, just as it ends with the strange child Winifred crooning to the rabbit, "Let mother stroke its fur then, darling, because it is so mysterious—." It is a mystery as an embodiment of vital energy, "magically strong," "demoniacal" in its resistance, "mad" in its swift changes of mood. In confronting it, Gerald and Gudrun participate in a mystery of another sort, an obscene rite of revelation and initiation, in which they become "implicated with each other in abhorrent mysteries." The power of the scene results from the intensity with which Lawrence renders both mysteries, and the intensity and depth of the psychic revelations are increased here by their impact on the characters, who themselves participate in "the mutual hellish recognition." Coming upon Gudrun struggling with the rabbit, Gerald sees, "with subtle recognition, her sullen passion of cruelty." The "unearthly abhorrent scream" of the rabbit as Gerald strikes it seems "to have torn the veil of her consciousness," and "she knew she was revealed." Gerald too is revealed, and the sense of viewing hidden inner depths is intensified by their juxtaposition with the outward surface, what these characters now know themselves to be with what they still pretend to be in their conventional words.

> "How many scratches have you?" he asked, showing his hard forearm white and hard and torn in red gashes.
> "How really vile!" she cried, flushing with a sinister vision. "Mine is nothing."
> She lifted her arm and showed a deep red score down the silken white flesh.

> "What a devil!" he exclaimed. But it was as if he had knowledge of her in the long red rent of her forearm so silken and soft. He did not want to touch her. He would have to make himself touch her, deliberately. The long, shallow red rip seemed torn across his own brain, tearing the surface of his ultimate consciousness, letting through the forever unconscious, unthinkable red ether of the beyond, the obscene beyond.
>
> "It doesn't hurt you very much, does it?" he asked, solicitous.

Only at the end does either make any overt acknowledgment of the fact that they are both now "initiate."

> "God be praised we aren't rabbits," she said in a high shrill voice.
>
> The smile intensified a little on his face.
>
> "Not rabbits?" he said looking at her fixedly.
>
> Slowly her face relaxed into a smile of obscene recognition.
>
> "Ah, Gerald," she said in a strong, slow, almost man-like way."—All that, and more." Her eyes looked up at him with shocking nonchalance.
>
> He felt again as if she had hit him across the face—or rather as if she had torn him across the breast, dully, finally. He turned aside.

Her words complete the strange bond which has been established between them. Gerald's response recalls the earlier slap she has given him after dancing before the highland cattle and looks forward to the last blow she will give, foreshadowing the final form their tangle of sadistic and masochistic compulsions will take. The scene thus performs the structural function which Vivas ascribes to the constitutive symbol: "It is a complex situation or scene . . . which gathers the significance of events preceding it and illumines the scenes or situations that follow. Yet it also develops a kind of self-contained intensity which gives it a stature almost like that of an independent poem, a powerful revelation."

This scene is as near as Lawrence comes in *Women in Love* to creating an actual scene of recognition, yet it is still far removed in function and import from the crucial scenes of recognition on which George Eliot's and James's novels so often turn. Recognition plays a lesser role in Lawrence because knowledge, especially conscious knowledge, is not as important a factor in his characters' development as the kind of relations they enter on a level which conscious knowledge can scarcely reach. Although Gudrun and Gerald do experience a recognition which is a crucial element of the rabbit scene, it is not in itself a crucial element in their subsequent development. It consists of a kind of intense awareness which is not really conscious, not the possible subject of thought. (It is Birkin who must attempt to deal with these mysteries consciously, conceptually, precisely because he does not, like Gerald, have "direct and personal" knowledge of them within himself.) Thus it is a recognition which offers no possibility for change but rather confirms the characters in what they already are. In terms of their subsequent development, the scene's crucial function is to place them definitively in their essential relation, to which their recognition is ultimately only incidental.

Because it achieves this symbolic definition, it is appropriate that "Rabbit" is located at the center of the novel, as is the famous symbolic scene in the following chapter, "Moony," where the relation of the other two major characters is presented. Like the rabbit scene, the one in which Birkin, unknowingly watched by Ursula, tries to destroy the reflected moon bears a complex relation to the novel's schematic patterns. The two pages which describe the stoning of the moon are probably the best example in all of Lawrence's works of his ability to create symbolic depth by rendering affective intensity. The description is from Ursula's point of view, but the intensity seems to reside in the moon itself: as Birkin throws the first stone, "it seemed to shoot out arms of fire like a cuttlefish, like a luminous polyp, palpitating strongly before her." Not satisfied, Birkin throws more stones.

> Then again there was a burst of sound, and a burst of brilliant light, the moon had exploded on the water, and was flying asunder in flakes of white and dangerous fire. Rapidly, like white birds, the fires all broken rose across the pond, fleeing in clamorous confusion, battling with the flock of dark waves that were forcing their way in. The furthest waves of light, fleeing out, seemed to be clamouring against the shore for escape, the waves of darkness came in heavily, running under towards the centre. But at the centre, the heart of all, was still a vivid, incandescent quivering of a white moon not quite destroyed, a white body of fire

writhing and striving and not even now broken open, not yet violated. It seemed to be drawing itself together with strange, violent pangs, in blind effort. It was getting stronger, it was re-asserting itself, the inviolable moon. And the rays were hastening in in thin lines of light, to return to the strengthened moon, that shook upon the water in triumphant reassumption.

The intense emotion, expressed in the medium of Lawrence's poetic prose, whose devises we have already examined (e.g., the assonance and alliteration of "the rays were hastening in in thin lines of light"), actually belongs to the two characters, Birkin's violent desperation and Ursula's shock, but it is contained in the image of the moon. Lawrence's ability to animate natural objects with an intense life of their own is again at work here, so that the tormented moon is at once a psychic correlative and an independent entity. The entire passage constitutes one of Lawrence's finest prose poems, even more detached from the narrative progression than the rabbit scene.

Yet its specific meaning is more dependent on context. Birkin prefaces his attack on the moon with the exclamation, "Cybele—curse her! The accursed Syria Dea!" which refers us back to his earlier meditation on woman as the Great Mother, desiring to merge rather than maintain separation in love, to absorb and dominate the male: "He had a horror of the Magna Mater, she was detestable." It is this aspect of Ursula which Birkin attacks in the archetypally female moon. He thus deliberately acts on a symbolic level, creating his own ritual for the expression of his feelings. The scene might therefore have been a simple allegory, one contrived by the character as well as the author, were it not for the intense feeling it contains, making Birkin's behavior the acting out of psychic conflicts which exist on a deeper level than his (or Lawrence's) ideas about them. Again, the scene is not one of recognition, though a kind of recognition follows it in Birkin's meditation on the alternatives of disintegration and "pure integral being" and his determination to try to achieve the latter in marriage to Ursula. The symbolic sense itself, however, is concerned not with recognition but with revelation, creating an intense, isolated moment in which not only the specific orientation but the enormous energy of the unconscious is made manifest. Although the scene's explicable meaning depends on the context of Lawrence's allegorical scheme, it develops a centripetal symbolic concentration which resists assimilation to a purely thematic function. As David Gordon remarks, such moments in Lawrence's novels "have symbolic energy far out of proportion to the purpose of furthering the narrative; they absorb us in and of themselves as revelations of states."

Despite the tensions which develop between the different components of Lawrence's mode, their collective effect is one not of incoherence but of increased richness and depth. His need to reveal unconscious states of being and to generalize their significance led him finally to create, in *Women in Love*, an original, highly symbolic fictional mode.

The Family Plot

Robert L. Caserio

In *Women in Love* Lawrence *looks* more reconciled to the surrender and negation of fatherhood and of a familial form of story, but after *The Rainbow* his self-division grows rather than lessens. Thus, in *Women in Love,* far from easily surrendering fatherhood, Lawrence is obsessed with the imagination and the pursuit of fathers, and he is arguably more obsessed as a result of the vehemence of his antagonism to them. Gerald Crich and his father are the next versions of Anton Skrebensky in Lawrence's fiction, and they are the scions of what is nothing less than an English House of Atreus, whose hereditary crime is unparalleled willfulness (of Gerald, for example, we know he was "that willful, masterful—he'd mastered one nurse at six months"). But in reading *Women in Love* we have always been misled by insisting that Rupert Birkin is Lawrence. Lawrence is no less Gerald's father and Gerald than he is Birkin; indeed he likely enough wants to be and feels that he is the *novel*'s "repressive central authority," the equivalent of the industrial magnate and the father-apparent of the Crich household. The power of *Women in Love* is harrowing because the struggle between Rupert and Gerald is Lawrence's struggle to subdue his own family plotting and to subdue and even destroy the Gerald in himself.

The Crich-figure, the allegedly repressive central authority, is analogous to the fathering (or mothering) authority in any novelist or storyteller because of the way the father shapes spontaneous appearances of the world into telling and objectified order. The vehicle of this

From *Plot, Story, and the Novel: From Dickens and Poe to the Modern Period.* © 1979 by Princeton University Press. Princeton University Press, 1979.

shaping is an analytic arrangement that masters the world's appearances and produces or engenders those appearances as plot and story. (We are again considering narrative reason, of course—a willful, active, relation-making component in it rather than a passively reflective component.) In the senior Crich, productive and reproductive shaping of the world is combined with unremitting paternalistic attention and personal sympathy: and unlike Tom Brangwen, Mr. Crich never questions his right to feel responsible, like a father, for ordering the world according to a shape he believes will best express and interconnect its parts. But Lawrence is afraid the productivity and sympathy of this fathering authority is a mask for a terror of death, for a will to master dread and vulnerability, for a panic in the face of meaninglessness and negation. Mrs. Crich sees this panic as her husband's "armor," his refusal to surrender not just to death but to life. Yet the senior Crich has so successfully exerted his shaping parental force that he is physically untouched by death. In one of the novel's most neglected but significant scenes, Mrs. Crich is roused to hatred by the resistance to vulnerability and death expressed by the face and flesh of her husband's corpse. She cries out to her children with "a strange, wild command from out of the unknown, . . . 'None of you look like this, when you are dead! Don't let it happen again.' "

We ought to read this remarkable scene as a projected panicky desire on Lawrence's part to dissociate himself from the father he identifies as the repressive central authority because he fears that he wants to be that authority himself. In fact, the scene is symbolic of Lawrence's anxiety that storytelling—narrative reasoning (even when humbled by being dissociated from imitation of action)—is implicated in democratic industrial forms of mastery. Mrs. Crich's command is that *storytellers* not "look like this," that they not give a vivid impression of life as the result of reproducing its contingencies and disruptions or its spontaneous absence of filiation in a form and in a reasoning that controls and masters these diverse phenomena, producing their meaning and making them tell in a hierarchized, centrally organized way. Such mastery gives an impression of life, but is indistinguishable from death. We always take Lawrence at his word, acknowledging that he wants no such mastering parenthood. But does Mrs. Crich's hysteria come from a resistance that is purely disengaged? If Lawrence's shaping authority in the novel is analogous to the will of the male Criches, can he surrender his own will to sire order and meaning through life's reproduction in the form of the novel? In wanting a brotherhood with Gerald—the master of a family and a social order of masters and slaves—Birkin (Lawrence's alleged spokesman) wants a brotherhood, a mutuality, that uses a family term to transcend both family and the intertwining of mastery with physical and cultural parenthood. Birkin's author wants this transcendence as a narrative form to write by and as an ethic to live by. Can he wrestle down and negate the Crich-figure in himself?

We can examine how the wrestling works out in two adjacent incidents in the "Continental" chapter of *Women in Love*. Among a crowd of Germans in their Alpine lodge, Rupert and Ursula and Gerald and Gudrun are dancing the *schuhplattel*. The dance becomes powerfully erotic, and Birkin takes his wife to bed to perform an unspecified sexual act that is new to her. "Wasn't it rather horrible," Ursula thinks, "a man who could be so soulful and spiritual, now to be so—she balked at her own thoughts: then she added—so bestial?" Ursula winces, but then she exults. "She exulted in it. She was bestial. How good it was to be really shameful! There would be no shameful thing she had not experienced." At the same moment, still below at the dance, Gudrun is ashamed to admit that Gerald is not monogamous, but, as she says, "naturally promiscuous. That is his nature." Later, in their room, Gerald, whom Lawrence describes as "glistening," asks Gudrun, "Who do you like best downstairs?" The motive of this question is not clear, and it begins a powerful and similarly unclear "strange battle between her ordinary consciousness and his uncanny, black-art consciousness."

What is this juxtaposition of the two couples about? What is its plot; what is the story that makes it tell? Lawrence appears to inhibit himself from *making* it tell. The licentiousness of the two men and the differing responses of the sisters to what they take to be male sexual brutality exemplify the narrative adjacency that puts a premium on the absence of ties, causations, motives, defining connections. Lawrence communicates here a texture of being prior to any ordering of it: an extravagance of blood, a random and momentary human flowering, a haze and shimmer with which even brutal eros glistens. And is not this moment of juxtaposition, in the haze that leaves connections open and disrupted, characteristic of the entire form of *Women in Love*? To answer affirmatively is to agree that the Lawrence who writes the novel *is* like the Birkin who does not want to shape life or to master its meaning by producing meaning out of the world or out of his darkly shimmering self. Yet to read *Women in Love* this way is to evade the truth behind each of these juxtaposed blood-flowerings of Lawrence's characters. We know as soon as we step back from the juxtaposition that not a single spontaneous shimmer is here without its conditioning cause or purpose, without its telling filiative connection assigned it by the author. Lawrence makes us know that Gerald is not "naturally" promiscuous, as Gudrun self-defensively wants to think; Lawrence insists we recognize that Gerald is promiscuous because he is the product of a society artificially willful and obsessed with production and mastery. His licentiousness comes from his inherited democratic-industrial fear of vulnerability and death. Lawrence insists we recognize as well that Ursula can freely bless her own shamefulness because she is free of Gerald's fears and also because she is free of the productive industrial complex Gerald controls and is also controlled by. Indeed Lawrence's plot forces upon us the idea that Birkin's lusts are due to his absence of defensiveness and that Gerald's are due to *his* protective armor. The sociological and psychological analysis of *Women in Love* is inalienable from its distinction; and its distinction is founded on the storyteller's authoritative use, analysis, and manipulation of causes and effects. And this is to say that the story and its power are founded irremovably on the shaping, narratively reasoning purpose of a story-teller who hierarchizes experience by designating its origin and its filiated strands and who fathers meaning by making life speak not randomly and spontaneously but under a compellingly purposeful direction.

Yet this fatherhood of analytic narrative reason and plot so troubles Lawrence that he must hand himself over to the defeat and negation of his own authority. It is not an exaggeration or distortion to speak of negation. Remembering Birkin's ethic of polarities, we may claim that Lawrence's narration is a polarized balance of the paternal-masterful mode and the mutual-yielding mode. But were Lawrence balanced between two narrative modes and not torn between them, not convinced that one must negate the other, we probably would not have *Women in Love*. We would certainly not have the grief and terror of the last chapter of *Women in Love*. The negation and the intense desire for it is clearly spoken in that chapter, in a passage completing a much earlier thought of Birkin's. The earlier thought is that

> at moments it seemed to [Birkin] he did not care a straw
> whether Ursula or Hermione or anybody else existed or did
> not exist. Why bother! Why strive for a coherent, satisfied

life? Why not drift on in a series of accidents—like a picaresque novel? Why not? . . . Why form any serious connections at all? Why not be casual, drifting along, taking all for
what it was worth?

The immediate but not the final answer to these questions comes
from Lawrence the storyteller: "And yet, still, he was damned and
doomed to the old effort at serious living." This means that Birkin is
doomed to making serious connections, to engendering relations if not
filiations, just as Lawrence feels himself "damned and doomed" to the
old effort at seriously mastering life by connecting and interrelating its
experiences in the form of family plot. But in the last chapter of
Women in Love this old effort is negated by Birkin's admission that to
care for any form of connection rather than any form of drift is not
worth the damning and dooming effort; the image of the glamorously
wasteful poppy is now tragically darkened. Rupert turns away from
Gerald's corpse. "Either the heart would break, or cease to care. Best
cease to care. Whatever the mystery which has brought forth man and
the universe, it is a non-human mystery, it has its own great ends.
Man is not the criterion. Best leave it all to the vast, creative,
non-human mystery." Lawrence adds, "it was very consoling to Birkin
to think this."

The final wisdom—and consolation!—of *Women in Love* is the
powerlessness of humanity, its distance from the creative engendering
of relations, especially filiative ones. The one parent Lawrence can
acknowledge in *Women in Love* is the nonhuman one. Humanity fathers nothing and masters nothing—and *this* absence and negation of
fatherhood is the tragedy of *Women in Love*. Our applause of mutualities in discourse covers up the fact that the end of filiation is *the* central
misery in Lawrence's novel. We are used to thinking of the novel as
presenting the end of filiation as a misery only because, from Birkin's
point of view, humanity will not recognize the need to end the family
plot. But this is not the truth. There are two stories about family plot
in *Women in Love*, and we keep reading only one. The one we habitually read tells us that at the level of form the family plot is finished: we
have instead of its hierarchizing action and narrative reason a fictional
discourse founded on mutualities and adjacencies. At the level of
content Birkin represents this new form turned into a moral ideal: he
wants the end of hierarchy in family and marriage, he wants the end of
the family plot as fact. But at the formal level the end of filiation, the

humbling of that kind of meaningful form, is a screen, hiding the desire that the creative mystery be human and be made compatible with an organization of plot that is as bent on the authoritative mastery of life and meaning as are Mr. Crich and Gerald.

It is not mutualities and adjacencies of form but family plot as form and narrative reason that gives us the *story* of *Women in Love*; if we take away that form, we are left with the adjacencies of vivid sensations and of Birkin's rhetorical insistencies, but then neither of them will be telling or significant. Birkin insists that genuine love is brotherly or brother-and-sisterly, and Lawrence hopes both the familial and the narrative structures of filiation will be moved aside for this kind of love. But the hope has persuasive force and meaning only because it is not a spontaneous poppy-like flowering. Without the exercise of fathering authority that in Lawrence compels experience to speak as he sees and shapes it, we would not be moved to consider the urgent need for a new mutuality in life and in narrative. But it is clear that Lawrence wants to accept the negation of his own creative and analytic power. The fathering impulse in Lawrence becomes a secret agency of plot, and he mourns it the more deeply in secret, the more openly he denies it. Just as we are used to identifying Lawrence with Birkin, we are used to talking about *Women in Love* as the product of repressed homosexuality. *Women in Love* is more likely the powerful product of a repression of a desire for fatherhood that will not be appeased by either the morality or the form of the end of filiation.

Women in Love:
The Ideology of Society

John Worthen

What did Lawrence want his novels to be, after *The Rainbow*? Lawrence, after expounding *The Rainbow*, said that he felt that he would write one more novel, and no more. He was sad, because he was a forerunner, like John the Baptist before the Christ, whose place it was to give up and surrender. . . . "So I suppose my achievement begins and ends with preaching the revolution of the conditions of life—why not?"

Murry made that diary note in February 1915, and *The Rainbow* had begun to incorporate something of that "revolution of the conditions of life" as Lawrence finished it during February and revised it from March till August. Its final social optimism is what Lawrence himself wished to communicate to the people of England in the summer of 1915. But by mid-October he had lost that optimism about the future of society; his magazine *The Signature* had failed to capture an audience, public meetings in a room above Fisher Street brought no success, and he found the unchanging pointlessness of the war a final demonstration of the end of man's purposive belief in society (and in himself). Cynthia Asquith noted in her diary: "the war he sees as the pure *suicide* of humanity—a war without *any* constructive ideal in it, just pure senseless destruction." He decided to emigrate to America, but on the November day when the Lawrences' passports arrived, he also heard that Methuen had surrendered to the police all unsold and

From *D. H. Lawrence and the Idea of the Novel.* © 1979 by John Worthen. Macmillan, 1979.

unbound copies of *The Rainbow*, had recalled all unsold copies from the bookshops, and would be facing charges of publishing an obscene book. The news must have come with depressing aptness; just as he was deciding not to work for England any more, his novel was charged with being unfit to be read by English people.

But the idea of going to America, which had emerged as a spontaneous reaction to the hopelessness of the war, gave way to a revised idea of community—of *rananim*. In November 1915 Lawrence began to meet a number of people "who have the germ of the new life in them" (Dec. 20, 1915), and whose enthusiasm for the idea and hostility to the war made him feel that a community abroad was a real possibility. Robert Nichols, Dorothy Warren, Philip Heseltine, Dikran Koumidjian, Suhrawardy, Aldous Huxley—all declared themselves potential settlers; and instead of the community being a kind of England-in-spite-of-itself (as planned in the spring) it became unmistakably an escape from the England which actually existed, and from the war. It was to celebrate a new life, a life lived apart from English society, the English past and the actual moment of history; it would be a self-sufficient community of souls achieving spiritual satisfaction in the only way possible to them. It represented (and continued to represent for all Lawrence's life) the appeal of a community which was outside English society as Lawrence had known it; it was to be a community outside history, time and place. Lawrence was obviously much attached to the idea of a complete escape; but without a revolutionary idea of society, such an escape had to exist outside the realm of all the things which attached him to his own time. It was an idealist sort of escape because it rested on the belief that individuals together could achieve what they could not achieve as members of conventional society. There was always an air of unreality about Lawrence's proposed *rananims*, both now and for the next ten years; they were really a response to the particular effects of the War, and for Lawrence they were a way out of the contradictory feelings which the War imposed on him. In the age of the mass authoritarian state, he wanted to assert the integrity of the free individual; but he also wished to create and live the life of a community. Caught between freedom which was illusory and involvement which was unbearably painful, he invented *rananim* as a means of bridging the gap between society and individual fulfilment; as such, *rananim* summed up the basic contradiction in Lawrence's response to his society and to himself as an individual: it offered relief from both.

By mid-November, the Lawrences had passports, a destination, and a colonising group. But they did not go. For one thing, the very idealism of *rananim* was something that, in the end, Lawrence always shied away from. For another, to leave the country one needed military exemption, and some of the group almost certainly would not have got it. Lawrence himself queued up at Battersea town hall to be attested for exemption, but left the queue before his turn came. "I must say," he wrote immediately afterwards, "I feel again a certain amount of slow, subterranean hope. . . . It is only the immediate present which frightens me and bullies me. In the long run I have the victory; for all those men in the queue, for those spectral, hazy, sunny towers hovering beyond the river, for the world that is to be" (Dec. 12, 1915). The men in the queue—the men for whom Lawrence has the victory— "were very decent." He obviously wanted to offer them more than a spiritual *rananim*: he felt more deeply attached to them. He abandoned the queue and with it the immediate prospect of America, and went to live in Cornwall.

His months in London had seen the end of his belief in "revolution" and in "doing anything" publicly—the end of his hope to change his society by other means than by his writing. Cornwall was, from the start, seen as more than a refuge; it was to be a creative centre, after all. Lawrence wrote to Katherine Mansfield: "We must begin afresh—we must begin to create a life all together—unanimous. Then we shall be happy. We must be happy. But we shall only be happy if we are creating a life together" (Dec. 30, 1915). Lawrence never answered the question of what actually could be created, in such a way; in the end, his only creation of "a life together" would be in the pages of his novels. *Women in Love* would be his finest rejection of society, his most complex statement of attitude to the prevailing ideology, his own most intense ideological statement: his realisation of the contradictions of his own position as man and writer. He wrote it in Cornwall, and it became more important than any community he had ever planned.

Community in the sense of being "unanimous" itself receded in importance very quickly. Throughout the autumn of 1915 Lawrence had been insisting to his friends on the importance of unanimity, and he had expressed his strongest hostility to the merely personal. "I am sick and tired of personality in every way," he had written to Katherine Mansfield (Dec. 12, 1915). But in Cornwall he gave up the corresponding insistence on unanimity of purpose as something which could transcend the merely individual; it was as if he were gradually stripping himself of those beliefs which had so far sustained his belief in community itself. Koteliansky must have written to him in the first week of January complaining that there was no real harmony between the proposed group of colonists; and in a remarkable reply Lawrence declared himself "willing to give up people altogether." "There is my intimate art, and my thoughts, as you say. Very good, so be it . . . I am not going to urge & constrain any more: there are no people here in this world, to be urged" (Jan. 6, 1916). And he told Katherine Mansfield that he was not going to "strive with anything any more—go like a thistledown, anywhere, having nothing to do with the world, no connection" (Jan. 7, 1916). That was clearly a reaction from his feelings the previous September, when the Fisher Street meetings were being planned, about working for change and not caring if people were hard to convince; but even if Lawrence felt temporarily relieved of the *care* for humanity which had dominated him the previous year, we can still see a contradiction between the insistent casualness of such a remark, and how he actually behaved during 1916. He wanted a kind of freedom from society and care, a kind of new, free individuality; but he also hated individuality, and remained a writer deeply concerned with the existing relation between the individual and his society. On the one hand, "I feel very estranged" (Feb. 24, 1916): on the other, "Yet still one can be an open door, or at least an unlatched door, for the new era to come in by. That is all" (Jan. 9, 1916). He declared himself uncaring, yet the idea of the new, of change, dominated him. He wrote to Ottoline Morrell at the start of February:

> The only thing now to be done is either to go down with the ship, sink with the ship, or, as much as one can, *leave* the ship, and like a castaway live a life apart. As for me, I do not belong to the ship; I will not, if I can help it, sink with it. I will not live any more in this time. I know what it is. I reject it. As far as I possibly can, I will stand outside this time, I will live my life, and, if possible, be happy, though the whole world slides in horror down into the bottomless pit.
>
> (Feb. 7, 1916)

We must realise that this was not a final, impassive declaration. It represents something that, for the rest of Lawrence's life and his career as a writer, remained possible for him. His description of feeling "as if my heart had once more broken" (*Phx II*) while looking down on the modern world from Monte Cassino in 1920 suggests the pain of such a separation. But most of all it could affect his writing deeply; his novels were henceforward written in a way that could always stand back from the world of men and the world of his own past experience. Lawrence was never blithe about the possibility of separation that opened up for him in 1916; standing "outside this time" was never simple, or desirable, or even possible for very long. But the artist who sometimes did stand outside his own and his culture's present and past starts here: the wanderer, the biting satirist, the exponent of new religions of body and spirit starts here.

It was also typical of him that within four days of such a letter, he should be collaborating with Philip Heseltine on plans for the private publication of important books—notably *The Rainbow*: "I myself believe that there is something to be done by private publishing" (Feb. 11, 1916). In such contradictions, we can understand Lawrence. He could no more give up the hope of changing people, of advancing society, than he could finally escape from that fundamental belief in progress and advance which had been one of his inheritances from his mother, and from the nineteenth century. And he could not escape from either the desire, or the job, of writing novels to express that belief. He might feel unutterably alienated, but he could still express that desire to affect people, to alter the course of their lives.

> I feel quite anti-social, against this social whole as it exists. I wish one could be a pirate or a highwayman in these days. But my way of shooting them with noiseless bullets that explode in their souls, these social people of today, perhaps it is more satisfying. But I feel like an outlaw. All my work is a shot at their very innermost strength, these banded people of today. Let them cease to be.
>
> (Feb. 15, 1916)

His new philosophical work *Goats and Compasses*, the revised *Twilight in Italy*, *The Rainbow* as written in 1915—all were works subversive of conventional ideology, shots at the conventional "innermost strength" because so totally opposed to conventional belief. "I want to blow the wings off these fallen angels. I want to bust 'em up. I feel that everything I do is a shot at these fallen angels of mankind" (Feb. 15, 1916) "No more adhering to society. I am out of the camp, like a brigand. And every book will be a raid on them" (Feb 17, 1916). It was probably the successful completion of the first half of *Goats and*

Compasses which gave Lawrence the confidence to say that he was, finally, "out of the camp." But "any man of real individuality tries to know and to understand what is happening, even in himself, as he goes along" (*Phx II*), he wrote in his Foreword to *Women in Love*; what he felt he had understood in the spring of 1916 was his own social role, for ever outside the conventional ideology of society—and yet strangely attached to that society, still. He had moved on from one social role, of self-made educator of feelings, the idealist exponent of advance, to another: that of critic and mystic. Bertrand Russell was the kind of writer he himself refused to be; Lawrence wrote to him that "One must be an outlaw these days, not a teacher or preacher. One must retire out of the herd and then fire bombs into it" (Feb. 19, 1916). Lawrence's antagonism to society does not often sound as absolute as this, and we need to understand it as the corresponding swing of the pendulum to that which had carried him into such fervent social hope in 1915. And the important thing even about those "bombs" was that they would make people realise things, and not simply destroy them. But never again would this particular pendulum swing so far back the other way. One of his major concerns for the rest of his writing life would be what place he had, as a writer; what relationship with society, what contact, what responsibility.

The Lawrences moved into their new home at Higher Tregerthen, near Zennor, in March; "a tiny settlement, all to ourselves" (Mar. 11, 1916). It may have been "to ourselves," but as soon as they were all settled, Lawrence began to write again. The mood in which he did so is summed up in a letter to Ottoline Morrell:

> One must forget, only forget, turn one's eyes from the world: that is all. One must live quite apart, forgetting, having another world, a world as yet uncreated. Everything lies in *being*, although the whole world is one colossal madness, falsity, a stupendous assertion of not-being.
>
> (Apr. 7, 1916)

That "other" world might in theory be brought about by a colony, a *rananim*; but it could also be something created by the novel which Lawrence was about to write. A novel could take its stand against the prevailing ideologies of both rigid class structures and democratic opinion; it could assert a new world, an uncreated world of the spirit. That same month, Lawrence wrote to Catherine Carswell that she was "so intrinsically detached, so essentially separated and isolated, as to be a real writer or artist or recorder" (Apr. 16, 1916); that suggests how important such a standpoint seemed to him as an artist in 1916. *Women in Love* shows both its author's attempt to adopt such a standpoint, and his ultimate failure to do so.

But, interestingly, the novel he first thought of writing was not the continuation of *The Rainbow* at all. The recent prosecution and destruction of the first part of that novel may have made the writing of its second part too tender a matter; at all events, Lawrence's mind went back three years, to that amazingly creative spring of 1913, and the half-finished novel he had come to call *The Insurrection of Miss Houghton.* He had stopped work on that novel because it seemed too outrageous to be published. That would not stand in his way in 1916. He wrote to Germany for the manuscript; he waited almost exactly a month for it. But in the middle of the war, it is hardly surprising that it never came. Sometime in the last ten days of April he began *Women in Love*, "the second half of *The Rainbow*" (May 1, 1916).

He had begun to wish to deny belonging to a culture, a country or a society, altogether: "I hate the whole concern of the nation. Bloody false fools, I don't care what they do, so long as I can avoid them, the mass of my countrymen: or any other countrymen" (Apr. 18, 1916). And yet only a week later he was engaged on the novel, and insisting that there was no inconsistency in his attitude:

> I am doing another novel—that really occupies me. The world crackles and busts, but that is another matter, external, in chaos. One has a certain order inviolable in one's soul. There one sits, as in a crow's nest, out of it all. And even if one is conscripted, still I can sit in my crow's nest of a soul and grin. Life mustn't be taken seriously any more, at least, the outer, social life. The social being I am has become a spectator at a knockabout dangerous farce. The individual particular me remains self-contained and grins.
>
> (Apr. 26, 1916)

But this novel, at least, does more than grin at the society of its production, just as its range and activity shows more than a "particular me" involved in it. Lawrence could write, "I feel I cannot *touch* humanity, even in thought, it is abhorrent to me." And yet he was writing a novel: "a work of art is an act of faith, as Michael Angelo says, and one goes on writing, to the unseen witnesses" (May 1, 1916). Faith meant faith in others sharing his standpoint, aware of their contradictions as he was aware of his, aware of both the pain of alienation and the danger of individuality. A novel is an act of faith in its capacity to communicate with its readers, and to be for them what it can be for its author.

But never had Lawrence been so certain that what he was writing would meet with little or no response in its potential readers. "Already it is beyond all hope of ever being published, because of the things it says" (May 1, 1916), he was saying within a week of starting it. "It is a terrible and horrible and wonderful novel. You will hate it and nobody will publish it" (Oct. 25, 1916), he told Pinker after it was finished; "It is enough for me that it is written, in this universe of revolving worlds" (Oct. 3, 1916). He was right about its prospects; no one would publish it for four years, and most people found it incomprehensible. Cynthia Asquith saw the TS in 1918, and we can consider her a potentially sympathetic ordinary reader; she wrote in her diary:

> It is interesting—painfully so, and full of extraordinary bits of stark writing, but what is it all about and *why*? It seems a *mis*application of such a wealth of strenuous analysing and writing. Surely he is delirious—a man whose temperature is 103?—or do I know nothing about human beings? It is all so *fantastic* to me and "unpleasant"—morbid to a degree. I don't know *what* to think about it.

Sixty years on, it is easy to forget just how difficult its first readers found *Women in Love*. Today's critics go through the book like lions through a paper hoop; critical guides exist in which the crooked is made straight and the rough places plain. But as late as 1930, as whole-hearted an admirer of Lawrence's genius as F. R. Leavis could complain that "To get through it calls for great determination and a keen diagnostic interest . . . never again does he come near to offering, as here, a parallel to the turgid, cyclonic disasters of Blake's prophetic books." In 1945 George Orwell felt confident that "with few exceptions Lawrence's full-length novels are, it is generally admitted, difficult to get through." Above all, *Women in Love* made its first readers feel that it was a mad book. *The Observer* headed its review "A Mad World" and commented: "page after page reads like the ravings of some unfortunate being subjected to the third degree." Rebecca West, for many the voice of the avant-garde, wrote that "many of us are cleverer than Mr. D. H. Lawrence and nearly all of us save an incarcerated few are much saner." *John Bull*—admittedly a special case—

remarked that "most of his characters are obviously mad." The *London Mercury* felt that "one would have to sweep the world before getting together such a collection of abnormalities," even John Middleton Murry, who was staying with the Lawrences when the book was first written, and who shared in discussions which found their way into it, remarked in his review that it was "five hundred pages of passionate vehemence, wave after wave of turgid, exasperated writing impelled towards some distant and invisible end; the persistent underground beating of some dark and inaccessible sea."

What did its readers find so hard? Fundamentally, like Cynthia Asquith they asked "what is it all about and *why*?" Those are still the right questions. *Women in Love* is a book whose relationship with the world of its production is particularly complex—as its author's own remarks about it might suggest; on the one hand, "most people won't even be able to read it" (Oct. 3, 1916), on the other he felt he had "knocked the first loop-hole in the prison where we are all shut up" (Oct. 11, 1916). In exactly the same way, in the book, Birkin both rejects society utterly—he would like "everybody in the world destroyed" —yet replies to Ursula, when she asks him "why do you bother about humanity?", "because I can't get away from it." And, as she sees, he wants to be a "Salvator Mundi." The novel, too, is committed and remains committed to the society of its production, both by being written as a publishable novel submitted to publishers in the normal way when finished, and by continually dwelling on the social worlds of twentieth-century England.

And yet, as a novel, it insists continually that people of heightened consciousness both should and do live in a different world. At one point Gerald asks Birkin "where's your special world?" Birkin answers: "Make it. Instead of chopping yourself down to fit the world, chop the world down to fit yourself. As a matter of fact, two exceptional people make another world. You and I, we make another, separate world." Birkin believes this, and the novel offers it as something we too can believe. The novel is designed to "knock a hole in the wall", just as Birkin feels that "to know, to give utterance, was to break a way through the walls of the prison"; the novel's foreword offers the book as a "passionate struggle into conscious being" (*Phx II*). Yet to understand that "conscious being" in yourself, or in the created characters, is to insist on another world from twentieth-century English society. The more we understand *Women in Love*, the more it serves to alienate us from the society in which we are reading it and understanding it. *Women in Love*, like all novels, is in a continually shifting relationship with the society of its production; it dramatises that society, it may even reflect it, but it also creates its own world; in this case, an insistently other world. Because although *Women in Love* seems to deal at great length with the society of its day, it works a vital transmutation upon the society it presents. To take a single example; the novel starts with two women sitting in a room discussing marriage. As has been pointed out, this is a starting-point reminiscent of a number of nineteenth-century novels. We seem to be in a world stressing moral choice and the opportunities of women in society. David Cavitch writes of the two sisters: "like vain or superior ladies in fiction of more than a century earlier they are afraid that all married men are bores and that married life will not sustain the sense of heightened significance, the romantic vividness, that they require in life." But "romantic vividness" certainly is not what these ironical young women desire. And four times in these first few pages we are told that one or the other of them is frightened. Cavitch says that they are frightened of the bad marriages they might make—men and romance being so incompatible. But the novel's stress goes far deeper than this: "in their hearts they were frightened." In the world of the Regency novel which Cavitch evokes, fear is an emotion which young ladies would experience about spinsterhood, not about marriage. Gudrun and Ursula's talk is light, flippant and clever; it is also obvious that they feel more than they admit. Three times, in fact, Gudrun tries to end the conversation; emphatically she does not want to pursue the ideas her sister offers her, about children, about being reckless, about their father. Both of them jump at the chance of going to see the wedding, as an escape from the crevasses which keep opening beneath the conversation.

We are told something of the origin of Ursula's fears first:

> As she went upstairs, Ursula was aware of the house, of her home round about her. And she loathed it, the sordid, too-familiar place! She was afraid at the depth of her feeling against the home, the milieu, the whole atmosphere and condition of this obsolete life. Her feeling frightened her.

She is conscious of the gap between her cheerful ironies and her fundamental feeling. The contrast is violent. Both sisters cope so well with conventionalities (or the lack of them), so elegantly and superciliously; but neither can face "this obsolete life." The novel has indeed offered us a scene reminiscent of the social intercourse of a Regency novel; it also suggests, immediately, that social life as Gudrun and Ursula experience it is both frightening and obsolete.

The sisters walk through Beldover—"a dark, uncreated, hostile world." Gudrun's reaction is that "It's like being mad, Ursula." Critics commonly distinguish Gudrun's reaction—which they see as bad—from Ursula's; the crucial thing is that, like the narrator, both sisters respond to the scene not as it is but in terms of the feelings which it provokes in them. Beldover is less described, than rendered in terms of heightened consciousness—terms which presumably made Cynthia Asquith write "delirious" and "*fantastic*" about the book's descriptions. It is not a mining village but a kind of hell through which Gudrun is led, as she asks what *her* world can be, if this is "the world." As in the first scene, what she says is different from what she actually experiences. She is actually shocked, bewildered and frightened, but she says: "It is like a country in an underworld. . . . Ursula, it's marvellous, it's really marvellous—it's really wonderful, another world. The people are all ghouls, and everything is ghostly." Words like "wonderful" and "ghouls" sound forced; but only in that way can she create her sense of "another world" and enjoy her fear. Later in the chapter, as the sisters watch the wedding party go into the church, she sees each person as "a complete figure, like a character in a book, or a subject in a picture, or a marionette in a theatre, a finished creation"; and we again see her almost consciously insisting on her world, on her right to *make* a world. We cannot simply say that Gudrun's view of Beldover is biased, or foolishly unaware of the social reality of the place; the narrator himself uses words like "amorphous," "aborigine," "brittle," "magic," "obsolete," to create *his* vision of the world, and those too are words describing the heightened consciousness of someone who finds this world an alien world, a species of hell. A phrase like "It's like being mad" would come as naturally from the narrator as from Gudrun. He shows us an ordinary cabbage stump, or a street, and we register it as an artefact of hell. "I think we've all gone mad," says Ursula in "Water-Party." "Pity we aren't madder," replies Birkin—and, again, the narrator would agree with him.

So when Gudrun sees Gerald, and thinks of him as "a young, good-humoured, smiling wolf," as someone who "did not belong to the same creation as the people about him," I suggest that we find Gudrun's language one of discovery and revelation. ("Am I *really* singled out for him in some way, is there really some pale gold, arctic light that envelopes only us two?")—not something we could judge inadequate. It is the language of someone discovering the mystery of another human being; the language of someone fated to a certain kind of experience: it has nothing to do with the way that people should (or do) behave in society. The novel's dreamlike quality comes from the way it turns the normal world into a species of hallucination—a vivid, unreal panorama. Beldover, "as if seen through a veil of crape," its chimney smoke rising "in steady columns, magic within the dark air," is a compelling vision of the real world turned unreal.

This is true, too, of an incidental aspect of the book to which the early reviewers and critics often drew attention, but which modern criticism largely ignores—the continual detailed description of clothes. Even chapters apparently cast in the mould of conventional realism instruct us to focus our attention on the unreality of the perceived world, and on the violence of our relationship with it. There is a vivid contrast between the brilliant clothes of the two girls, the blackened place, and the hostile inhabitants. In "Coal-Dust" two labourers watch the girls:

> They saw the two girls appear, small, brilliant figures in the near distance, in the strong light of the late afternoon. Both wore light, gay summer dresses, Ursula had an orange-coloured knitted coat, Gudrun a pale yellow, Ursula wore canary yellow stockings, Gudrun bright rose, the figures of the two women seemed to glitter in progress over the wide bay of the railway crossing, white and orange and yellow and rose glittering in motion across a hot world silted with coal-dust.

The repetitive second sentence helps create the phantasmal appearance of the girls; they are glamorous in the full sense of enchanting. Rebecca West, in 1921, noted the "sheer meaningless craziness" of the "extraordinary descriptions of women's clothes," Murry said much the same thing, the *Saturday Westminster Gazette* reviewer (who had fun with the whole novel) thought that " 'Enter a purple gown, green stockings, and amber necklace' would do for a stage direction if *Women in Love* could ever be dramatised." It is right to notice the clothes; they are clearly meant to be noticed. They individualise the characters against the world. The labourers watching Gudrun and Ursula are, strictly, in another world—and that everyday world is both temporal (with its momentary pang of lust) and unreal. Gudrun's clothes are, appropriately, the most often described, just as her keeping of herself to herself (very different from Birkin's conception of singleness) always isolates her and keeps her disturbingly separate. She leaves the Pompadour café with Birkin's letter, and just where we might have expected a sentence or two about her feelings, we get this:

> She was fashionably dressed in blackish-green and silver, her hat was brilliant green, like the sheen on an insect, but the brim was soft dark green, a falling edge with fine silver, her coat was dark green, lustrous with a high collar of grey fur, and great fur cuffs, the edge of her dress showed silver and black velvet, her stockings and shoes were silver grey. She moved with slow, fashionable indifference to the door.

We learn, half a page later, that she is "frozen with overwrought feelings" and violently angry with Birkin: "Why does he give himself away to such *canaille*?" Giving herself away is precisely what Gudrun will not do; the description offers a curious mixture of Gudrun exposed (even the taxi which collects her has lights "like two eyes") and Gudrun concealed. Halliday's reading of the letter aloud obviously touches her deeply, by what it says as much as by how he reads it: "I want to go," is her instant reaction. She conceals herself by leaving, and crushes the letter in her hand as she goes; but she is also making a public gesture. So she presents herself only as a "form"; glossy, fashionable, the greens and silvers and blacks like a shell over her feelings. The "sheen on an insect" confirms this sense; she is deeply concealed against the moment of public exposure. The description of her clothes is Lawrence's way of suggesting her true tension at such a moment, the terror of her isolate self, always buried yet always fearing exposure, always in danger of giving itself away.

The first part of the novel is constantly aligning the experience of the individual consciousness against the moeurs of established society, and suggesting that such opposition is the norm of contemporary life. Gudrun and Ursula both go to a wedding, but, like the people taking part in it, seem hardly aware of the social reality of the ceremony. The wedding breakfast in chapter 2 turns into a discussion of race and nationality, hinging on the individual's "pleasant liberty of conduct." Chapter 3, "Class-Room," lacks all sense of the social reality of teaching children in a school; education is discussed entirely in terms of the arousing of an individual's consciousness. In chapter 4, "Diver," we do get a momentary sense of what is possible for a man, but not for a woman, in society; but that chapter too finds its centre in a discussion of the independence of the proud individual, set like a swan against the geese of society. In chapter 5 we find Birkin's assertion that "first person singular is enough for me"—and so on. We have been in a number of carefully distinguished social worlds, but their vividness is given the quality of a dream rather than of a reality; the individual's consciousness makes them dreamlike.

This is particularly odd since in this novel, more than in any of his others, Lawrence creates a wide spectrum of society and shows us what Gudrun feels to be "the whole pulse of social England." But the novel is not so simplistic as to set the claims of the individual consciousness against the threat of the social world, and say simply that the individual's only hope is to depart from the mass and cleanse himself (as *St Mawr* was to say in 1925). *Women in Love* is a greater novel than *St Mawr* because it creates situations in which individuals would like to be free, and where freedom is not so easily attained; where a tension between liberation and constraint (social, sexual, economic, cultural) is continually reinforced. We can see such a tension in Gudrun in the Pompadour, where it makes her brittle to the point of fragility. Birkin, throughout the novel, would like to be free, independent and self-satisfying: "The old way of love seemed a dreadful bondage, a sort of conscription . . . he wanted to be single in himself, the woman single in herself." Rolling in primroses, he prefers the "new-found world of his madness" to the "regular sanity" (as well he might). "Why form any serious connections at all? Why not be casual, drifting along, taking all for what it was worth? And yet, still, he was damned and doomed to the old effort at serious living." He is as separate as a man can be, from the social world; his job keeps him unlocated and he feels he can give it up at any moment—"tomorrow perhaps." Yet it is his doom, his fate, to be attached to the world. When he defines for Ursula what he means by "the last thing one wants," he says "I don't know—freedom together," itself a paradox and a limitation of himself. Love haunts him, yet seems a "conscription"—a word which in 1916 could only suggest the recently (and for England uniquely) introduced military conscription: the state's ultimate binding of the individual. He expresses his commitment to Ursula by giving her rings; yet also insists that he bought them only because "I wanted them." He insists that people do not matter, yet it is his commitment to have dinner with Hermione and say goodbye to her which provokes the quarrel in "Excurse." The novel shows Birkin moving in and out of phase with the social world; the same man who rolls naked among the primroses also "looked a failure in his attempt to be a properly dressed man" in Halliday's London flat. Proud single-ness can only be suggested in "freedom together," and the idea of going away with Ursula instantly suggests his need of still further people.

> "To be free," he said. "To be free, in a free place, with a few other people!"
> "Yes," she said wistfully. Those "few other people" de-pressed her.
> "It isn't really a locality, though," he said. "It's a per-fected relation between you and me, and others—the perfect relation—so that we are free together."

Lawrence in fact gives Birkin notably more sense of commitment to others than he ascribed to himself; just before starting the novel, he remarked that "It is scenery one lives by, but the freedom of moving about alone" (Mar. 25, 1916)—and the "few other people" never materialised for him.

It might be argued that the paradoxes of the novel are simply confusions, reflecting contradictions in its author. If *Women in Love* were another sort of novel, then they might well be. But *Women in Love* is a very carefully constructed experimental novel, designed to elicit paradox rather than fall helplessly into it. Its very structure is a refusal of simple narrative progression; its clear-cut, often unlinked chapters follow not the sequence of a particular narrative but the progress of particular concerns—like individuality, freedom, love and consciousness. Birkin's confusions are the necessary links in a chain of thoughts, as are Ursula's insistencies. The novel is constructed to elicit from its characters the complexities attendant upon their advanced lives; it interweaves theory and experience, idea and counter-idea, knowing and being. "All vital truth contains the memory of all that for which it is not true" (Dec. 19, 1914), Lawrence once wrote; the same could be said of a novel like *Women in Love*. A simple narrative necessarily suggests the progress of thoughts to a conclusion; the characters of *Women in Love* (and we ourselves) only reach realisations, are not aware of truths. When we find Birkin both as obstinate and as unclear at the end of the novel about what he wanted from Gerald, as he had been at the beginning, we don't need to blame a confusion in Lawrence's own heterosexual and homosexual impulses (as, for instance, Scott Sanders does); we need to realise that Gerald is a focus for Birkin of his need for more than a single intimacy, his need for "other people," his desire for "another kind of love"; it is something the novel has dramatised, not something it has reached a conclusion about or is offering as a truth.

The novel as a whole, in fact, is asking what kind of freedom—or individuality—is possible for a man like Birkin; his attachment to Gerald has the force of a necessary, if unwanted, bond. The Pompadour crowd are distinguished by their deliberate freedoms; when Gerald asks about them "All loose?" Birkin replies "In one way. Most bound, in another." Gerald himself tells the Pussum that he is "afraid of being bound hand and foot" before she gives herself to him; but she is loose with Gerald only to ensnare Halliday. The young men in Halliday's flat flaunt their freedom from convention by being deliberately nude; but they are people trapped in their own "repetition of repetitions." What Birkin offers Ursula is never as free as his own discovery, in chapter 8, of "the new-found world of his madness": "he would be free in his new state." "As for the certain grief he felt at the same time, in his soul, that was only the remains of an old ethic, that bade a human being adhere to humanity." But he has just been knocked over the head by Hermione, and his experience offers a temporary relief from caring rather than a final break; never again does Lawrence allow him to be so free of the "old ethic." Indeed, both Birkin and the narrator insist on the "connection with life and hope" which human beings need. But Birkin's primary insistence is on his doctrine of "free, proud singleness"; that kind of individualism is his primary recourse against the society which he hates. "He said the individual was *more* than love, or than any relationship."

At least, this is what Birkin would like to think. It is an assertion made in a context which modifies it; Birkin is, in fact, neither free nor proud nor single. Right at the end he breaks down over the death of Gerald: "He should have loved me"—and we hear about his "heart's hunger," his *need* of "eternal union with a man too." His assertion of singleness, and aristocratic pride, is not allowed to stand; he whimpers, he wipes his face "furtively." And the freedom which has been one of his keynotes is severely qualified, too; Birkin and Ursula may be going abroad again, but this novel ends with them both back in England, at the Mill; this is what their exercise of freedom has come to. Ursula had insisted in "Excurse" on taking "the world that's given—because there isn't any other" while Birkin wanted to "wander away from the world's somewheres, into our own nowhere." And in chapter 26 he had demanded that his surroundings should be "sketchy, unfinished, so that you are never contained, never confined." Back at the Mill, in the rooms Hermione had so lovingly helped furnish, he and Ursula are "somewhere" with a vengeance. They may only be staying "a week or two" but the irony is necessarily final; the novel ends there. "Freedom" has been asserted only in a tension against "constraint," for Birkin as well as for Gudrun.

The novel, in fact, creates a vision of society which continually denies the simple truths Birkin tries to cling to. Its relationship with society is crucial; we cannot say that the novel inevitably reflects the society of 1916, because a novel never simply reflects a society. Its relationship with the ideology of society is both that of product and creation. A novel always creates a society, a world—in the case of *Women in Love* it does so very obviously—and is itself a piece of ideology which refers back to the society of its production, but which also can carry the ideology of its society in a new or different direction. Lawrence himself felt, when he had finished *Women in Love*, that he had indeed created a world:

> I know it is true, the book. And it is another world, in which I can live apart from this foul world which I will not accept or acknowledge or even enter. The world of my novel is big and fearless—yes, I love it, and love it passionately. It only seems to me horrible to have to publish it.
>
> (Oct. 3, 1916)

But the world he felt he had created—"big and fearless"—isn't necessarily the world he had actually created, and its relationship with "this foul world" is more complex than he suggests. Parts of the book indeed, come so close to the real world of 1916 that I do not think we can separate them from it as easily as Lawrence himself felt he could, in that letter; yet they, too, have been transmuted into something very different from the objective social reality from which they spring. The bulk of the chapter "The Industrial Magnate," for instance, purports to be an account of the coal industry in the generation before Gerald assumes control of the family business, and of the changes he institutes in it. Lawrence was able to draw on a good deal of personal knowledge in his account of the industry and the owning family. His father had worked in Brinsley pit as an employee of Barber, Walker and Co., the Barbers being the family Lawrence drew on most extensively in his account of the Crich family. Every year, on Boxing Day, the miners' children were invited to Lamb Close, the Barber family home, and we know that Lawrence himself went at least once. He also met Philip Barber at least once, too, but knowledge of the family and its doings was common gossip. *Sons and Lovers* and some sketches of the mining industry written in 1912 ("The Miner at Home," "Her Turn," "Strike Pay") suggests his knowledge of the industry, and how he kept in touch with local affairs even after he left Eastwood; we find him asking William Hopkin to write him letters "full of good old crusty Eastwood gossip" (Dec. 18, 1913), and his sister Ada certainly told him how things were going in the mining industry.

And it is, furthermore, generally assumed that "The Industrial Magnate" is a truly historical account of change. Various critics refer to "Lawrence's criticism of pre-war England," to Gerald as "the epitome of his civilisation," "the representative and embodiment of European industrial civilisation"; the "world of the novel" has been described as " 'social England' at a specific point in history, a moment of debacle." Those critics do not appear to consider that the history of England outlined in "The Industrial Magnate" is unlike any history they could have read elsewhere. As Lawrence describes them, the changes Gerald introduces into the mining industry represent "a new world, a new order"—and as such language suggests, the "new world" in this novel is not an objective social reality but a facet of consciousness. The Crich miners are described as "satisfied" by the changes Gerald makes, but not because their working conditions are improved or their wages put up. They are satisfied in their souls, though "their hearts died within them."

> The working of the pits was thoroughly changed, all the control was taken out of the hands of the miners, the butty system was abolished. Everything was run on the most accurate and delicate scientific method, educated and expert men were in control everywhere, the miners were reduced to mere mechanical instruments. They had to work hard, much harder than before, the work was terrible and heartbreaking in its mechanicalness.

Such a passage is a strange conflation of truth and fantasy. In the extensive modernisation of the mines at the end of the nineteenth century, more electricians and engineers were employed in an increasingly mechanised industry. Yet the vision of total change is utterly untrue to history; and it is certainly untrue that most miners had to work "much harder" after mechanisation. Lawrence goes on: "And yet they accepted the new conditions. They even got a further satisfaction out of them." What he means by "satisfaction" is reduction, self-immolation in the machine; he is talking about souls, not about working selves. Lawrence's own later description of the modernised industry at Moorgreen pit as he saw it in 1925 is surely far more realistic:

> The pit is foreign to me anyhow, so many new big build-ings round it, electric plant and all the rest. It's a wonder even the shafts are the same. But they must be: the shafts where we used to watch the cage-loads of colliers coming up suddenly, with a start . . . while the screens still rattled, and the pony on the sky-line still pulled along the tub of "dirt," to tip over the edge of the pit-blank.
> It is different now: all is much more impersonal and mechanical and abstract.
>
> *(Phx)*

That is the reaction of a man naturally puzzled and alienated by an enlarged industry, nostalgic for the past. But what he had described in "The Industrial Magnate" is the counterpart of his analysis of emotions in the novel; "sensation" in sexual relations is re-created in industrial terms. Gudrun, both repelled and fascinated by Gerald as he spurs his horse at the railway crossing, is satisfied in the same way as the miners are satisfied by Gerald's demonstration of power, and Lawrence is surely very acute about such a response. That does not mean that the miners of England behaved as "The Industrial Magnate" says they did; the novel is, once again, creating in its own terms the consciousness of the age.

The chapter is, in fact, more concerned with myth than with history. When Lawrence describes the difference between Gerald and his father, he is not directing our attention to a change in the general outlook of industrial management between 1880 and 1914; he is describing his sense of a fundamental change in Christian society in post-Renaissance Europe. The Crich family is a mythic analogue, not an historical reality. Lawrence is primarily concerned with spiritual change, and presents the miners as the willing participants in that change: "Gerald was their high priest, he represented the religion they really felt. . . . They were exalted by belonging to this great and superhuman system which was beyond feeling or reason, something really godlike." Lawrence is defining his novel's interest in society—the destruction of man as a social being. Gerald and his colliers are seen committing themselves to "the great social productive machine": "This was a sort of freedom, the sort they really wanted. It was the first great step in undoing, the first great phase of chaos, the substitution of the mechanical principle for the organic." Such freedom is like that of the London Bohemian circle; freedom without any belief in "the ultimate unison between people—a bond" which, Birkin insists, is the only thing which holds the world together. "The Industrial Magnate" chapter creates a picture of a world from which the individual must free himself, and one to which he is almost fatally attached; it is the world of modern consciousness.

That was the extent to which Lawrence was prepared to take his novel. Of all the novelists writing in 1916, he was in a unique position to describe the actual conditions of industry as the working man experienced them. Yet he not only ignored or transmuted his knowledge of the actual conditions, he ignored events like the South Wales miners' strike of July 1915—which was a stand taken against a nation at war, against the power of a centralised government, and against the power of local coal-owners. The novel's strike is considered metaphysically, not economically. He ignored the wartime plan for nationalising the coal industry—something his own political programme of February 1915 had looked forward to, as a necessary step in the revolutionising of society. The worlds he is concerned with in "The Industrial Magnate" are created worlds, not realistic ones.

The final location of the novel is the Tyrol; but this, too, is hardly a realistically created setting. The Tyrol is constantly described as an "other" world; it is the most extreme "other" world of the novel, and affects all the characters deeply. Even while journeying to it, Ursula is conscious of leaving behind "the old world"; she means England, which, like the continent glimpsed from the train, is only "the superficial unreal world of fact." She and Birkin are making a "final transit out of life"; they lose all sense of "the old world," being concentrated not "on the world, only on the unknown paradise." Ursula feels herself "projected" out of the world she knows—the world of her own past—which starts to feel like an obstacle to her newly developing, alienated self. Her past self starts to feel like "a little creature of history, not really herself."

At the guest-house, the process is carried still further. "She wanted to have no past"; and after her initial fears of this "different world," she develops an unnatural self-confidence—something really rootless. The Alps are "the navel of the world" and give the people an "other-world look"; they intoxicate Ursula with "a conceit of emotion and power," releasing inhibition and stimulating consciousness. For Gudrun the place is "her place," cutting her off finally from responsibility to Gerald (or anyone), and from any possibility of creative relationship. She reaches her own final isolation here. Gerald responds to the freedom with a release of energy, skiing as a man "projected in pure flight, mindless, soulless, whirling along one perfect line of force." Only Birkin cannot bear it—or could not, without Ursula; this world, more real than real, frightens him. Its dream of freedom is so powerful, glimpsed in the house itself, set "in the midst of the last deserted valleys of heaven . . . deserted in the waste of snow, like a dream."

England and the past vanish for all the characters—but particularly for Ursula. The place seems to offer the freedom which the real world denies, to be indeed the "nowhere" which Birkin wanted, to be a release from the 'other world' of home: "That old shadow-world, the actuality of the past—ah, let it go!" Once Ursula had insisted on "the world that's given—because there isn't any other." Now she too has a vision of "a new world of reality":

> What had she to do with parents and antecedents? . . . She
> was herself, pure and silvery, she belonged only to the
> oneness with Birkin, a oneness that struck deeper notes,
> sounding into the heart of the universe, the heart of reality,
> where she had never existed before.

Ursula certainly does not want to spend the rest of her life in the Tyrol. Her vision of a separate, individual self, at one with Birkin, is rather different from his original idea of life with those "few other people." And yet, once and for all, she seems to have released herself from the "old world" which Birkin, too, wants to be free of; she can now match him, and together they can just "wander off'—or, as the novel presents them, live in their own world.

Gudrun, too has a final vision in the Tyrol:

> If she could but come there, alone, and pass into the in-
> folded navel of eternal snow and of uprising, immortal
> peaks of snow and rock, she would be a oneness with all,
> she would be herself the eternal, infinite silence, the sleep-
> ing, timeless, frozen centre of the All.

It is a vision both hallucinatory and repulsive; but she is not actually going to put her boots on and start climbing. The vision, like so much of the novel, mediates between a real, actually apprehended world, and the world of a fulfilling imagination. The novel is an attempt to convince us that such experiences of the world are, for us, indeed our truest experience of it; we truly "make the world we do not find."

And each character in the novel makes such a world of his or her own. More obviously than the other characters, Gerald has such a world, back in England; but he gives it up without a pang and apparently receives neither telegrams nor anger from Shortlands. The Tyrol offers him an utterly satisfying physical world, but all he can do (as ever) is "see this thing through." "There must be a conclusion, there must be finality"; his kind of unsatisfied physical and psychic longing finds its conclusion in self-abnegation and a desire to kill Gudrun—and so have her "finally and for ever." His longings revolve inwardly and tempt him, as Gudrun too is tempted, into a "oneness with all," a final relief and sleep; but as he actually *does* set off upwards after half-strangling her, we know that his only destiny is to become that "sleeping, timeless, frozen centre of the All" which was the culmination of Gudrun's vision. He wants to "come to the end—he had had enough," but all he can do is simply keep going—and we should remember the mocking irony from chapter 4 of "he's got *go*, anyhow." But where does the "go" go to? Finally, into nothingness; "he slipped and fell down, and as he fell something broke in his soul, and immediately he went to sleep." Such an ending is a marvellous combination of realism, vision and parable; the world Lawrence makes for Gerald is a perfect interpenetration of the worlds of fact and spirit; his physical death is a spiritual tragedy.

Gudrun's "world" is harder to define; yet she, too, struggles to achieve one. As an artist, she remains unattached to place; Beldover, London, Sussex, Shortlands are all simply resting places for her. She flirts with the idea of marriage to Gerald, with "what he represented in the world"; but her genuine knowledge of the "whole pulse of social England" makes her recoil in irony from the idea. All she can believe in—and always ironically—are the "perfect moments" of her life. She rejects the whole of conventional society, in withering irony. That makes her sound like Birkin, but unlike him she has no vision of ideal relationship, or of a way of life. She is, we could say, entirely unspiritual, and there is a price to be paid for that. She can construct fantasy worlds with Loerke, and as an artist she can insist that "my art stands in another world"; but that has to be enough for her. The novel leaves her wondering "*wohin?*"—"she *never* wanted it answered"—unattached, unbelieving, terrified, playful as and when she needs to be, perfectly cynical; surviving. She finds a solution to the problem of living in this world posed by the novel; her individuality hardens into obstinate personality. But she survives, as it is her fate to.

Ursula begins the novel with a place to which she belongs (unlike Gudrun), a job, a past she has grown up from; only her future is empty. She ends the novel with no past and no desire for anything in the present which "this world" can give her. Her future is, simply, to live with Birkin, to "come down from the slopes of heaven to this place, with Birkin." Reality is a matter of belonging "only to the oneness with Birkin"; from that point onwards, she can wander the world with no trace of regret. When, indeed, Gudrun offers Ursula her own arguments about accepting the world as it is—"the only thing to do with the world, is to see it through" (an argument terrifyingly true for Gerald)—for "you can't suddenly fly off on to a new planet," Ursula replies, "One has a sort of other self, that belongs to a new planet, not to this. You've got to hop off." It is an answer Birkin would be proud of. And that is where the novel leaves her.

Birkin, of course, is the most consistent believer in new worlds in the whole novel. Early on, he plays with the idea of "a world empty of people, just uninterrupted grass, and a hare sitting up"—though we should note how his unworldly words are followed shortly afterwards by the careful "carpeting" of his rooms. But the world he wants most often is the "world of proud indifference" with Ursula, where he is "a strange creature from another world," where they can "wander away from the world's somewheres, into our own nowhere." I have already suggested both the extent to which they want to do that, and the degree to which the vision is unrealised. Birkin's faith in "the mystery" and in living with Ursula in a world of their own—and in ceasing to care, as he ceases to care about everything in the world except Gerald and Ursula—remains central in the novel, a provocative centre which is true to the presentation of the world as the novel creates it.

With his novel finished—"another world"—Lawrence hardly felt like publishing it: "It seems such a desecration of oneself to give it to the extant world" (Nov. 20, 1916). Such remarks apparently confirm his sense of the artist's necessary detachment; in the novel it is Loerke who feels that the work of art "has no relation to anything outside that work of art," and we are told by Gudrun that Loerke "*is* an artist, he is a free individual" because he has "an uncanny singleness, a quality of being by himself, not in contact with anybody else, that marked out an artist to her." Lawrence obviously knew what it was to feel that. And yet, if *Women in Love* survives as a significant novel, it must be because it succeeds in having a relation with the world outside it; as Ursula puts it, "The world of art is only the truth about the real world." And Lawrence also knew what it was to feel "a gnawing craving in oneself, to move and live as a real representative of the whole race" (Dec. 23, 1916). The artist perhaps has to feel that. Critics write about Lawrence's misanthropy as if it must have damaged him profoundly as a novelist: "you cannot make fiction out of hatred for humanity." There is no evidence that Lawrence ever tried to; it is also true that while writing and revising *Women in Love*, he felt utterly alienated from the world of England. The kinds of purposes he had felt in 1915, culminating in the vision of a new world which took over the end of *The Rainbow*, were things which would never get into his novels again. The foreword he wrote for *Women in Love* in 1919 sets out to make it sound a wholly personal work, in fact: "This novel pretends only to be a record of the writer's own desires, aspirations, struggles; in a word, a record of the profoundest experiences in the self" (*Phx II*). Most readers probably feel that there are moments when it reads primarily as a reflection of the "deep, passional soul" (*Phx II*) of its author; and yet *Women in Love* also demonstrates an author having the confidence that the soul he confronts in himself is also "a real representative of the human race." And through his creation of the novel's characters we see him living out the contradictions of his own position as an artist.

In its stress on the individual, *Women in Love* stands as one man's response to his own deliberate social isolation, as the record of his own "struggles." But it is also representative of a hatred of the ideology of his society; it creates individuals in worlds of their own, making the happiness they cannot find, standing against the social world which has reduced human society to the ugliness of Beldover, the repetitiveness of the Pompadour, the insentient mental fibre of Breadalby and the human tragedy of Shortlands. *Women in Love* makes no sort of compromise with the problems it obviously causes for its readers; it transmutes social reality into the play of heightened consciousness, and says that *that* is our true world. It insists on vision, on impracticality, on the deathliness of social bondage and liberated personality alike; but it is a novel which also creates worlds of other people and other attachments.

It represents an idea of what Lawrence in 1916 thought both art and individual consciousness should be; but it also creates imaginative worlds full of life, not only of individuality. Eschatological critics make much of the titles Lawrence considered using for it, in the later summer of 1916: *Dies Irae, The Latter Days*. It was not, however, a weaker sense of England's doom that made him revert to the earlier title *Women in Love*. Such a title suggests the free play of irony, the colloquial inquiringness, which underlies the book. It isn't *Men in Love*—though it might have been: but are they in love? What are the women in love with—themselves? *Does* Gudrun love Gerald? Does Ursula not love Birkin "too much" (as he insists)? In such ways, the title opens up the world of the book quite undogmatically; and in such realism is the strength which keeps it alive as a novel. It is the strangest of Lawrence's books; it shows the real world falling into phantasmagoria; but like the African sculpture so often discussed, it is a high pitch of art, it is a desperate creation of the almost unbearable.

The Teller Reasserted: Exercisings of the Will in *Women in Love*

Gavriel Ben-Ephraim

> "You'd have to have it your own way, wouldn't you?"
> [Ursula] teased. "You could never take it on trust."
> [Birkin] changed, laughed softly, and turned and took her
> in his arms, in the middle of the road.
> "Yes," he said softly.

The covenant between man and God, whose traditional sign shines so hopefully at the end of *The Rainbow*, is shattered in *Women in Love*. The mood of the latter novel is harsh and pessimistic, nearly despairing, with humanity written off as "dry rotten" and "full of bitter, corrupt ash." The final impression *Women in Love* makes is of a bleak apocalypse, a world ending in cynicism and freezing; this is partly because it presents hopelessness with superb force, while its hope is full of qualification and lacks conviction. The teller analyzes the destructive relationship of Gerald Crich and Gudrun Brangwen with a savage certainty of perception, but brings less realization to his portrait of the marriage between Rupert Birkin and Ursula Brangwen. The reason for the discrepancy is that whereas tale and teller unite in the depiction of Gerald and Gudrun, the description of Birkin and Ursula is self-contradictory, a dramatic illustration of tale/teller division in Lawrence's fiction.

The corrosive death struggle between Gerald and Gudrun is admirably articulate. Symbol, action, dialogue, and—most impressively—the alterations of the hidden underself, the carbon of character, all

From *The Moon's Dominion: Narrative Dichotomy and Female Dominance in Lawrence's Earlier Novels.* © 1981 by Associated University Presses.

advance this tale of master and slave reversals, of the will to power answering the will to be overpowered. The power-alternations between Gerald and Gudrun seem evenly distributed, with each character taking his turn at ascendancy. But a close examination reveals that the mind-dominated Gudrun has a cold integrity of self and cruel survival-capacity, making her a far stronger figure than the will-driven Gerald. Gudrun's final indifference protects her, giving her a frigid intactness, while Gerald's pressing needs make him vulnerable, a sacrifice to the violent winds blowing through *Women in Love*. Gudrun's being is perverse, but Gerald's is disintegrative. Between the two of them, he is the one condemned; all his manipulations of power are but attempts to counter his underlying weakness. In their demonic way Gerald and Gudrun present the fundamental Lawrencian tale: the interaction between an ontologically strong woman and a less individuated man. (Their entanglement remains Lawrence's most vivid example of the destructive potentialities of such a relation.)

Where Ursula and Birkin are concerned, the teller distorts the respective strengths-of-being the two characters show as the tale reveals an ontological imbalance between them. Ursula incarnates a pure, mysterious wholeness of being: she is suffused with "a golden light" that indicates self-integrity. Birkin, in contrast, is implicated in the social and individual corrosion that causes a degradation of being. The tale shows Ursula providing the solution to this degradation: Birkin has a chance of swimming clear of the "river of dissolution" that threatens to flood their doomed society by aligning himself with her. The conception of Ursula as antidote to dissolution is worked out carefully in sustained character-development and realized symbolic incidents. Yet the teller seems to avoid this inherent conclusion, this natural proclivity of his novel. *Women in Love* works against itself, and the contradiction is revealed by a contrived, overinsistent tone, when Ursula submits her healthy soul and will to the more corrupted Birkin. Describing this submission, the teller attributes redemptive properties to the same force of corruption that is throughout depicted as destructive. And this contradiction is at the heart of the tale/teller problem in *Women in Love*: for while the negative implications of corruption are fully dramatized by the tale, its positive powers are only asserted by the teller. The narrator is required to make the assertion in his effort to justify the unequal consummation-scene that climaxes the novel. There the teller unthrones the *magna mater*, putting Birkin in a superior position while claiming to show equality. It is a dual tension, opening gaps between both tale and teller and tale and the reader's knowledge of experience. Hence the willed subjugation of Ursula to Birkin leads to discrepancies that mar this otherwise very great work.

The central technical accomplishment of *Women in Love*, like that of *The Rainbow*, is the apprehension of the carbon of character. But where *The Rainbow* is based on a myth of carbon, the technique of *Women in Love* is that of carbon-symbolism. In the earlier novel Lawrence analyzes the way in which the fundamental experiences of life—birth, marriage, sex, and death—register on the obscurely emotional, instinctive self; *The Rainbow* is a recapitulation of the life-cycle as it is perceived on the carbon level. In *Women in Love* the teller replaces these general renderings of carbon-states with sharp, specific images of inner being; he hypostatizes the carbon-self, giving it various, concrete forms. This gives *Women in Love* a febrile vividness lacking in its predecessor. (On the other hand, Lawrence's extended exposition of his characters' underselves—tedious as it sometimes becomes—gives *The Rainbow* a sustained depth unmatched elsewhere in his fiction.)

More consistently than Ursula and Birkin, Gudrun and Gerald are described and developed through the effective device of carbon-symbolism. An early example of an image that serves as an objective correlative for a psychic essence of being is evoked by Gudrun; she is observing the light that seems to gleam about the handsome industrialist, Gerald Crich: "There was something northern about him that magnetized her. In his clear northern flesh and his fair hair was a glisten like sunshine refracted through crystals of ice. And he looked so new, unbroached, pure as an arctic thing. . . . 'Am I *really* singled out for him in some way, is there really some pale gold, arctic light that envelops only us two?' "

Gudrun and Gerald are united in frigid incandescence, but not only they are "enveloped" by the pale light. We learn from a later interior monologue of Birkin's that such light represents a kind of psychic disintegration. The monologue, stimulated by the memory of an African statue, grimly prophesies the "universal dissolution" of mankind, asserting that the process will take two forms: African and Arctic:

Thousands of years ago . . . in these Africans . . . the desire for creation and productive happiness must have lapsed,

> leaving the single impulse for knowledge in one sort, mind-
> less progressive knowledge through the senses, knowledge
> arrested and ending in the senses. . . . There is a long way
> we can travel, after the death break: after that point when
> the soul in intense suffering breaks, breaks away from its
> organic hold. . . . We fall from the connexion with life and
> hope, we lapse from pure integral being, from creation and
> liberty, and we fall into the long, long African process of
> purely sensual understanding, knowledge in the mystery of
> dissolution. . . . It would be done differently by the white
> race. The white races, having the Arctic north behind them,
> the vast abstraction of ice and snow, would fulfil a mystery
> of ice-destructive knowledge, snow-abstract annihilation.

In the "African" way the personality is disrupted: the "outspoken mind" which looks to ideas and values is abandoned and so is the chance for creative self-expansion. Incapable of enlargement, the organism turns to reduction, depleting itself by feeding on its own frictional sensations; the self becomes a closed envelope, experiencing only itself and, because trapped in the corporeal body, finally having nothing to experience but its own decomposition. Hence, it lives according to "knowledge in disintegration and dissolution, knowledge such as the beetles have, which live purely within the world of corruption and cold dissolution." The "white races" of the arctic way partake of the same principle of dissolution. Here too the self is enclosed, receives its satisfactions within the enclosure, and is diminishing by the limitation. But this more complex process occurs against the backdrop of a "vast abstraction." The point seems to be that Western man, with his intellect-based culture, is held within his self-conscious mind; he therefore experiences his body through a self-observing consciousness that holds sensation at one remove. (The Arctic and African processes are closely related, but not identical.) The way of "ice-destructive knowledge, snow-abstract annihilation" is the way of mind that makes coldly abstract ideas and images out of experience, yet is incapable of going beyond the experience of the corruptible self. It thus ends with a frigid apprehension of disintegration. In both the African and Arctic ways, the organism loses contact with the pleasure that comes from the creative, reproductive functions of organic life, and seeks the subtler sensations found in "knowledge in dissolution and disintegration." (Hence Birkin reasons that the phallus is not the source of the deeper "sensual realities," and implies that the anus holds the most mysterious and profound "sensual understanding.") The African or Arctic process is one of corruption because it only conceives the dying curve of the organic cycle, and has lost all response to the engendering, growing, or blossoming aspects of organic life.

Gudrun's image (I ask the reader's indulgence for my digression) links Gerald and herself to the qualities connected to the Arctic way. (The image, as should be obvious, describes a distortion at the level of the carbon-of-character.) As presented in the novel, both characters' lives involve a cold savoring of dissolution, and most critics have seen them as equally participant in a frigid attenuation of self. Yet there is an essential distinction between Gudrun's and Gerald's ways of being. Gudrun experiences through a fanciful mind that keeps reality remote and frees her for a frostily indifferent view of life. Gerald participates in a different version of the Arctic way: he concentrates on sensation controlled in the self and imposed on others by a dominating will. The difference between living according to the manipulating mind or the dominating will is this: the will needs responding objects on which to exert itself, while the mind can content itself with its own perceptions and creations. This distinction explains Gerald's greater dependency in the relationship and accounts for his final defeat in the destructive struggle between the two characters.

Gudrun's vitality-denying life-of-the-mind is familiar, recalling many earlier (and subsequent) Lawrencian women. Prefigured by the "negative" Lettie, the Lettie-as-Eve in *The White Peacock*, Gudrun's true predecessor is Helena, the fanciful heroine of *The Trespasser*. Gudrun consistently alters the world in her transforming imagination, because, like Helena, she fears physical reality. An artist, Gudrun disarms the surrounding world by rendering it into a simplified creation of her own making; she mentally places people, organizing and clarifying their importance to her until each is "like a character in a book, or a subject in a picture, or a marionette in a theatre. . . . She knew them, they were finished, sealed and stamped and finished with, for her. There was none that had anything unknown, unresolved." Gudrun, as her sister Ursula notes, has a penchant for the miniscule: "she must always work small things, that one can put between one's hands, birds and tiny animals. She likes to look through the wrong end of the opera-glasses, and see the world that way." In her art, as in her mind, Gudrun prefers the small things that fit neatly into her ordering imagination. When reality nevertheless stubbornly intrudes on her, as when some colliers' wives call derisively after the well-dressed young woman, her fancy becomes murderous: "She would have liked them all annihilated, cleared away, so that the world was left clear for her."

Gudrun feels a perplexing attraction-repulsion toward her native mining-country: "Why had she wanted to submit herself to it, did she still want to submit herself to it, the insufferable torture of these ugly, meaningless people, this defaced countryside? She felt like a beetle toiling in the dust." The scarab or dung-beetle is associated with waste matter and hence with the "corruption and cold dissolution" that signifies the slow reduction of organic life to death; the beetle is a sign of the ultimate debasement of material life. In a kind of carbon-permutation, Gudrun becomes a "beetle" temporarily. Immersing herself in the "gritty" defacement of industrial corruption, she becomes a beetlelike forager in technological wastes. The masochistic submersion in ugliness satisfies, in some perverse way, Gudrun's craving for mind-stimulation. Yet Gudrun withdraws from the actuality of the blighted landscape. Self-protectively, she tries to mitigate the inherent force of the mining-scene by turning it into a creation of fancy. Taking something genuinely demonic, she reduces it to the make-believe demonism of her imagination: "It is like a country in an underworld. . . . it's marvellous, it's really marvellous. . . . The people are all ghouls, and everything is ghostly. Everything is a ghoulish replica of the real world."

Exposing herself to frightening phenomenon, she finds excitement and develops resistance. She is drawn to Gerald Crich because the Nordic brutality of his presence suggests a twisted stimulation: "His gleaming beauty . . . did not blind her to the significant, sinister stillness in his bearing, the lurking danger of his unsubdued temper. . . . She really felt this strange and overwhelming sensation on his account, this knowledge of him in her essence, this powerful apprehension of him." This masochism should not be confused with self-destructiveness; the violence Gudrun perceives in Gerald promises macabre additions to the spectrum of her experience.

Violence is Gerald's central, typifying characteristic. Through Gerald, Lawrence develops a daring view of industrialism as the product of the aggressive psyches of disordered men. In Gerald's hands, technology is a gigantic apparatus for punishing external nature. His punitive instrument is the *machine*, which serves to effect his will on a universe he regards as an eternal antagonist. The relevant question Gudrun asks about Gerald, "where does his *go* go to," finds its answer in Gerald's struggle to engage and subdue his environment. His is the energy of will, the energy that imposes itself; and he applies "the latest appliances" in order to overcome nature: "There were two opposites, his will and the resistant Matter of the earth. And between these he could establish the very expression of his will, the incarnation of his power, a great and perfect machine, a system, an activity of pure order, pure mechanical repetition, repetition *ad infinitum*, hence eternal and infinite." Gerald uses the machine to blight the green earth, to bow nature in mechanical service. The persistent automatic-motion Gerald worships, moreover, is a concretization of his own driving will to power. The machine is a primary carbon-symbol for the wealthy young industrialist, master of the midland collieries and overseer of the corruption Gudrun finds so perversely magnetic. The cold light she descries in him is, at least on one level, the harsh glare of burnished metal.

In his social views, Gerald is an instrumentalist: he equates a man's importance with his function, his role within the great progressing machine-society: "the idea was, that every man was fit for his own little bit of a task—let him do that, and then please himself. . . . Only work, the business of production, held men together. . . . Apart from work they were isolated, free to do as they liked." Denying the social significance of the private self mechanically bifurcates the human personality. In Gerald himself, the public and private selves mirror each other with cruel precision. The unity in these two parts of him shatter his theories about the detachability of the working self from the sexual self. Gerald's own experiences suggest that the instrumentalization of the social man is part of the dehumanization of the whole man.

Gerald's relationship to Minette, a dissipated model and member of the degenerate café society Gerald meets through Birkin, shows the destructive similarity in his professional and personal lives. Minette's appeal for Gerald recalls Will's attraction to the Nottingham working-girl in *The Rainbow*: Gerald is drawn toward an abusable woman who gives him the illusion of omnipotence: "He felt an awful, enjoyable power over her. . . . For she was a victim. . . . He would be able to destroy her utterly in the strength of his discharge." But the slavish foulness about Minette contributes an aura lacking in the relationship in *The Rainbow*; she brings in the true note of corruption, and here is the common element between Gerald's ways of working and loving. In his work, Gerald receives satisfaction from the effective application of a subduing will that spreads corruption. In his lovemaking, he

receives pleasure by immersing himself in corruption in order to dominate it: he thus finds his sensations, not through the body, nor the
mind, but through the will: "Her inchoate look of a violated slave,
whose fulfillment lies in her further and further violation, made his
nerves quiver with acutely desirable sensation. After all, his was the
only will, she was the passive substance of his will." In social functioning or sex Gerald abuses whatever is under his volitional power.

Minette herself, like the rest of the Pompadour Café group, is
involved in sensual dissolution. Birkin describes Minette's liaison with
another member of the group, Halliday, as an African connection, "a
return along the Flux of Corruption, to the original rudimentary
conditions of being." Minette incarnates African corruption as she
indicates the nature of Gerald's sensuality. Because he knows that
Minette has shared his own way of sex, Gerald recoils from her: "he
must go away from her, there must be pure separation between them."

Similarly, the primitive statue he observes in Halliday's flat is a
symbol for evaded aspects of himself. Birkin, who frequently assumes
the role of Gerald's intellectual mentor, explains the significance of the
carving: " 'it is an awful pitch of culture, of a definite sort.' 'What
culture?' Gerald asks, in opposition. He hated the sheer barbaric thing.
'Pure culture in sensation, culture in the physical consciousness, really
ultimate *physical* consciousness, mindless, utterly sensual.' " Gerald
himself is one step away from this level of reduction. But the statue,
whose significance for Gerald parallels the beetle's relationship to Gudrun, is a reminder that the "Flux of Corruption" pervades and taints
those who enter it. Receiving sensual corruption into the mind or will,
the receiver becomes corrupted. Gerald does not live for pure "physical consciousness," but he is devoted to his own kind of will-based
"culture in sensation." His resentment of Minette and the statue indicate his self-deception, his refusal to understand that the sensuality of
corruption draws him inevitably into the knowledge of disintegration.

We can both equate and distinguish between Gudrun's and Gerald's ways of dissolution. Gerald actively creates sensation-through-
corruption, while Gudrun is passively excited by the same process. But
both are stimulated by the forces that reduce organic life. Gerald and
Gudrun share an ability negatively to affect nature itself, to project and
extend their perversions *into* the circumambient universe instead of (in
the familiar, positive Lawrencian pattern) being healed *by* it. A series of
vivid animal-scenes communicate Gudrun and Gerald's mutual, vi-
ciously effective, need to disrupt the organic dignity of living things.

In the first of these scenes Gerald bullies his "red Arab mare" into enduring the chaotic passage of a seemingly endless train:

> He bit himself down on the mare like a keen edge biting home, and *forced* her round. . . . He held on her unrelaxed with an almost mechanical relentlessness, keen as a sword pressing into her. . . . The eternal trucks were rumbling on, very slowly, treading one after the other. . . . The connecting chains were grinding and squeaking as the tension varied, the mare pawed and struck away mechanically now, her terror fulfilled in her, for now the man encompassed her; her paws were blind and pathetic as she beat in the air, the man closed round her, and brought her down, almost as if she were part of his own physique.

Here is the typical product of Gerald's energy—the transformation of the organic into the mechanical. Her spasmodic pawings reveal how the mare's integrity has been usurped. Gerald terrorizes the animal until it is unable to function from its own centers of being: he subordinates the horse to the locomotive, forcing the creature to emulate the machine. At the same time, the animal becomes an extension of Gerald's own rigid automatism. A man more often controlled by his will than able to control it, Gerald is in this sense as "mechanical" as the creature he subdues. Gerald's bearing down on the mare is charged, also, with sexual implications; "the bright spurs . . . pressing relentlessly" join with the sexual suggestiveness of the train itself to imply a sadistic violation. This implicitly sexual violence brings Gudrun, who observes the incident together with Ursula, to the point of swooning: "The world reeled and passed into nothingness for Gudrun, she could not know any more." But she soon regains herself: "When she recovered, her soul was calm and cold, without feeling." Even Gerald's brutality, though it briefly fills her mind with overwhelming sensations, fails lastingly to affect her cold control.

A scene where Gudrun teases a herd of bullocks reverses Gerald's brutalization of his mare. The beasts frighten Ursula, but Gudrun dances insinuatingly close to the animals, expressing her fearless independence before them. She is excited by the animal's physical force, which she acknowledges. But her movement puts *her* in control; she stuns and confuses the bullocks, subordinating their lurking power to her imagination by turning them into manipulated figures in her dance-fantasy:

Gudrun, with her arms outspread and her face uplifted, went in a strange palpitating dance towards the cattle . . . her breasts lifted and shaken towards the cattle, her throat exposed as in some voluptuous ecstasy towards them. . . . The cattle . . . ducked their heads a little in sudden contraction from her, watching all the time as if hypnotized, their bare horns branching in the clear light, as the white figure of the women ebbed upon them, in the slow, hypnotizing convulsion of the dance. She could feel them just in front of her, it was as if she had the electric pulse from their breasts running into her hands. Soon she would touch them, actually touch them. . . . Oh, they were brave little beasts.

When Gerald appears, calling out to break the animals' mesmeric spell, Gudrun scatters them in a final gesture that leads to their diminishment: "she lifted her arms and rushed sheer upon the long-horned bullocks . . . they ceased pawing the ground, and gave way, snorting with terror . . . galloping off into the evening, becoming tiny in the distance, and still not stopping."

The ensuing struggle between Gerald and Gudrun, ostensibly concerning the bullocks, is really about the extent of Gerald's potency of will. The cattle, which belong to Gerald, are a metonymy for his maleness. He insists on their formidability, bringing out Gudrun's defiance. Though she had admired Gerald's dominance from a distance, Gudrun invokes her own stories of violence when the industrialist becomes palpably overbearing:

"You think I'm afraid of you and your cattle, don't you?" she asked.

His eyes narrowed dangerously. There was a faint domineering smile on his face. . . .

She was watching him all the time with her dark, dilated, inchoate eyes. She leaned forward and swung round her arm, catching him a light blow on the face with the back of her hand. . . .

And she felt in her soul an unconquerable desire for deep violence against him. . . . She wanted to do as she did, she was not going to be afraid. . . .

He recoiled from the slight blow on his face. . . . For some seconds he could not speak, his lungs were so suffused with blood, his heart stretched almost to bursting with a great gush of ungovernable emotion. It was as if some reservoir of black emotion had burst within him, and swamped him.

"You have struck the first blow," he said at last, forcing the words from his lungs, in a voice so soft and low, it sounded like a dream within her. . . .

"And I shall strike the last," she retorted involuntarily, with confident assurance. He was silent, he did not contradict her.

Both characters are overwhelmed by the dark, demonic feelings they inspire in each other, but there is a marked distinction. Gudrun, intoxicated with violence as she is, acts effectively. She strikes a blow just heavy enough to warn Gerald that he is forbidden to interfere with her. Gerald is too overcome by uncomprehended emotions to respond easily. Gudrun is calculating within the unstated hatred that submerges them, whereas Gerald is "swamped" (revealing word) by it. At a crucial point in the encounter he is without self-governance (a man who would be foolish if he were not so dehumanized), while she seems consciously diabolical.

Gerald is similarly "swamped" by his emotions in a chapter, "Water-Party," that sees him literally sink beneath the surface of Willey Water, the Crich family's private pond. Water is clearly associated with death and disintegration in *Women in Love* (compare Birkin's disquisition on the "dark river of dissolution"). Gerald therefore explains both literal submersion and submersion in his uncontrolled emotional self: the dark masses of water reflect and extend his own "ungovernable" waves of feeling. A series of chapters advance the relationship of Gerald and water, revealing that he lacks the integrity of ego to defy that annihilating element. In "Diver," first of all, he shows a superior mastery over Willey pond, enjoying a splendid isolation amid the "grey, uncreated water" he feels as his true element. But already in "Sketch-Book" the matter is complicated, for there Gerald's clumsy wilfulness costs him his dignity, preventing him from sharing Gudrun's remoteness from the muddy pond. In "Water-Party," Gerald senses that the cold depths suggest his inescapable fate: "it's curious how much room there seems, a whole universe under there; and as cold as hell, you're as helpless as if your head was cut off. . . . When you are down there, it is so cold, actually, and so endless, so different really from what it is on top, so endless—you wonder how it is so many are alive, why we're up here." And "Snowed Up" describes the culmination of Gerald's relationship to water, the element which adumbrates his inner chaos, and to which he grows increasingly close until, finally, he dissolves in the frozen waters of the snowy Alps. In a subtle way, Gerald's very rigidity consigns him to watery disintegration: the suggestion is that the man who holds himself together most rigorously is the man most likely, in the end, to come apart.

The scene involving Bismarck, the Crich family's great, white rabbit, is a blood-rite, a pact in destruction made by Gudrun and Gerald. The rabbit itself, in its blind, unthinking savagery, symbolizes the souls of the two human beings in this scene: here Gudrun, Gerald, and Bismarck are all *one:* " 'God be praised we aren't rabbits,' she said in a high, shrill voice. The smile intensified on his face. 'Not rabbits?' he said, looking at her fixedly. Slowly her face relaxed into a smile of obscene recognition." Gerald's mauling of the beast, and the bloody scratches it scores on the arms of both Gerald and Gudrun, create a grotesque version of Birkin's *Blutbrüderschaft:* the swearing of eternal loyalty between man and man becomes a swearing of eternal viciousness and violence between man and woman. Gudrun's and Gerald's understanding has a metaphysical aspect. Gerald swoons before a mystical essence of evil, a demonic version of the life-giving "Beyond" of *The Rainbow:* "The long, shallow red rip seemed torn across his own brain, tearing the surface of his ultimate consciousness, letting through the for ever unconsciousness, unthinkable red ether of the beyond, the obscene beyond."

In all three of the major animal-scenes Gudrun gives, at some point, a cry like a seagull's caw. The narrator also uses the seagull's scream to typify Ursula in one of the moon-scenes describing her annihilation of Anton Skrebensky. The aural-visual image is eerily successful, with an effectiveness that defies explication. But it is clear that the figure shows woman at her most horrible: a heartless, voracious creature. The seagull is a scavenger that lives off the battered leavings of the sea, and the sea is the element that reduces men of insufficient self. The equating of Gudrun and the seagull is one of many indications that Gudrun will outlive Gerald, that despite their "mutual hellish recognition," theirs is a hell in which the woman survives the man. Indeed, at points Lawrence makes explicit that underneath it is Gudrun who has the vanquishing force: "Gudrun looked at Gerald with strange, darkened eyes, strained with underworld knowledge, almost supplicating, like those of a creature which is at his mercy, yet which is his ultimate victor."

A chapter called "Death and Love" develops the difference between Gudrun's and Gerald's ways of being. The chapter describes two closely related subjects: the death of Gerald's father, Thomas Crich, and the subsequent intensification of Gerald's relationship with Gudrun. From his ideologically confused but utterly resolute father, Gerald learns to live by the principle of unrelenting will. Initially, even death seems to have no influence on the two strongly-resolved men: "And the father's will never relaxed or yielded to death. . . . In the same way, the will of the son never yielded." But, eventually, Thomas Crich's dying graphically reveals the limitations of human power. Watching his father's pitiful helplessness erodes Gerald's belief in the omnipotence of mortal violation—but the new awareness costs him his own rigid self-integration: "as the fight went on, and all that he had been and was continued to be destroyed, so that life was a hollow shell all round him, roaring and clattering like the sound of the sea . . . he knew he would have to find reinforcements, otherwise he would collapse inwards upon the great dark void which circled at the centre of his soul."

Losing his father, Gerald feels the "fearful space of death" within himself. Confronting the emptiness previously hidden by his deceptive self-assurance, Gerald now turns, with all the pathos of Will's fumbling need for Anna, to Gudrun:

> Something must come with him into the hollow void of death in his soul, fill it up, and so equalize the pressure within to the pressure without. . . . In this extremity his instinct led him to Gudrun. . . . He would follow her to the studio, to be near her. . . . He would . . . aimlessly pick[ing] up the implements, the lumps of clay . . . looking at them without perceiving them. And she felt him following her, dogging her heels like a doom.

As a result of his redoubled need, Gerald draws Gudrun to him in their first physical embrace. The contact has an assuaging effect as she becomes the "reinforcement" of being he requires: "he seemed to be gathering her into himself . . . drinking in the suffusion of her physical being, avidly."

Gerald is capable of the suspension of ego the teller refers to when he describes "melting" or "flowing" or "passing out" into the "darkness" (the "darkness" is the area beyond self-consciousness). But Gerald's self-loss consists of the absorption of one ego by another—it is a merger based on weakness; he takes Gudrun into himself, imbibing her as a means of restoring his enfeebled being: "His arms were fast around her, he seemed to be gathering her into himself, her warmth, her softness, her adorable weight, drinking in the suffusion of her physical being, avidly. He lifted her, and seemed to pour her into himself, like wine into a cup."

As for Gudrun, her ability to "swoon" and "pass away," "exquisite" while it briefly lasts, soon yields to her assertive, circumscribing ego. Coming back to consciousness Gudrun turns self-forgetting physical intimacy into an aggressive mind-intimacy. She gathers Gerald, through the tactile sense, into a mind that disintegrates all the mystery he brings from the darkness:

> There seemed a faint, white light emitted from him, a white aura, as if he were a visitor from the unseen. She reached up, like Eve reaching to the apples on the tree of knowledge, and she kissed him. . . . This was the glistening forbidden apple, this face of a man. . . . She wanted to touch him and touch him and touch him till she had him all in her hands, till she had strained him into her knowledge. Ah, if she could have the precious *knowledge* of him.

Eve is an apposite image for Gudrun. There is a parallel here between Lawrencian and Christian thought; in both world views original sin is the desire to know the unknowable; to transgress the prohibition against forbidden knowledge. For the Judaeo-Christian tradition the "unknowable" is the total moral wisdom implied by the knowledge of good and evil. Such knowledge is commensurate with God's omniscience, but it leads man to self-consciousness, shame, and guilt. Eve's desire *to know*, in its *hubris*, destroys the innocent, oblivious sensuality she shared with Adam, and brings, in its stead, the burden of self-awareness. For Lawrence the "unknowable" is the partner in the love-relationship. Intellectually apprehending another ego is intruding on a separate self that should remain inviolate and mysterious. Moreover, such knowledge destroys the possibility of redemptive self-forgetting.

The teller shows that Gudrun and Gerald want to imbibe and absorb one another. Gerald tries to take Gudrun into his very being and find protection against the void. Gudrun, the Eve-figure, attempts to take Gerald into her mind, to ingest him cognitively. Yet the two characters should not be equated. He is the weaker, for he looks to her for life itself; she is the uglier, for she feeds off him like carrion, picking at his body for stimulating knowledge that feeds her mind. Using imagery that recalls Ursula, the narrator describes Gudrun as a vulturelike creature of destruction: "How much more of him was there to know? Ah, much, much, many days' harvesting for her large, yet perfectly subtle and intelligent hands upon the field of his living, radio-active body. . . . Her hands, like birds, [w]ould feed upon the fields of his mystical plastic form." There is cruel irony, then, in Gerald's looking to Gudrun for support. He comes to her in all his pressing ontological need—but instead of being completed, he is to be devoured.

Gerald, however, is a willing victim, preferring a see-saw of annihilation to isolation. When Gudrun fails to appear for three days, he is overcome by an urgent drive for union with her. In a daze of "somnambulistic automatism" he stumbles toward her home. Yet there is an unconscious deliberateness in the movement, indicative of the connection between dependency and bullying. Because Gerald is incapable of being without her, Gudrun is unable to resist him. This is a dominating dependency to which Gudrun must submit: "She knew there was something fatal in the situation, and she must accept it."

The passages describing their first sexual consummation are vivid almost to the point of unbearability.

> And she, she was the great bath of life, he worshipped her. Mother and substance of all life she was. And he, child and man, received of her and was made whole. . . . The miraculous, soft effluence of her breast suffused over him, over his seared, damaged brain, like a healing lymph, like a soft, soothing flow of life itself, perfect as if he were bathed in the womb again. . . .
>
> He buried his small, hard head between her breasts and pressed her breasts against him with his hands. And she with quivering hands pressed his head against her, as he lay suffused out, and she lay fully conscious. The lovely creative warmth flooded through him like a sleep of fecundity within the womb. Ah, if only she would grant him the flow of this living effluence, he would be restored, he would be complete again. . . . Like a child at the breast he cleaved in-

> tensely to her. . . . He was glad and grateful like a delirium,
> as he felt his own wholeness come over him again, as he
> felt the full, unutterable sleep coming over him, the sleep of
> complete exhaustion and restoration.

In two of the novel's most resonant and disturbing carbon-symbols, Lawrence presents Gerald as both a foetus and an infant. (We remember the African statue he hates reminds Gerald of a "foetus.") A powerful need to revert to the womb exists within him alongside an equally insistent desire for mother-son unison-in-dependence that is surely Oedipal in its origin. The dual image unites in a complex depiction of a fragmentary ego, a partial man. Thus Lawrence provides a context for the problem of Gerald's deficiency of being (the context is amplified by the suggestive, if unelaborated, tensions between Gerald and his mother, Christiana Crich). Moreover, the womb-imagery, with its evocation of the amniotic fluid, subtly refers to Gerald's complex relationship to water. The attraction to water includes a desire for womblike security that is not only regressive but destructive, since what is life for the embryo is death for the man. (In general, Gerald's infantilism is the underside of his aggression. His brutality may thus express frustration at severance from an earlier union; indeed, brutality is a way of *forcing* merger.) But here unconsciousness replaces violence to ease Gerald's pain, for it allows him a simulacrum of the full, assuaging fusion. Beneath the subterfuge of his aggression, he longs for this comforting maternal flood and the dissolution of identity. Yet this unconsciousness, so paradisal for the moment, looks ahead to his death. Gerald's mind, tortured by the pain of separation, and a self-smothering need for fusion, eventually moves toward its own extinction.

The infant-foetus image is a brilliant example of the carbon-symbol technique that reveals parts of being below the perceivable personality. The technical success of the Gerald/Gudrun sections of the novel is based on this technique (as *The Rainbow* depends on the carbon-myth for its power). It is a notable demonstration that when Lawrence is technically successful he describes the struggles between a man of weak ego and a woman of superior ego-strength; it is arguable that Lawrence's style breaks down—as in *The White Peacock, The Trespasser, The Lost Girl* and *The Plumed Serpent*—when he tries to insist on ontological parity, or on male supremacy, in the man-woman relationship. This supports the conclusion that imbalance characterizes Lawrence's fundamental apprehension of males and females, and that a narrative describing this imbalance in action is the authentic tale he has to tell.

The brilliant description of Gerald's regressive core-of-being is matched by an equally acute rendering of Gudrun's carbon-self:

> She was exhausted, wearied. Yet she must continue in this state of violent active superconsciousness. She was conscious of everything—her childhood, her girlhood, all the forgotten incidents, all the unrealized influences and all the happenings she had not understood. . . . It was as if she drew a glittering rope of knowledge out of the sea of darkness, drew and drew and drew it out of the fathomless depths of the past, and still it did not come to an end, there was no end to it, she must haul and haul at the rope of glittering consciousness, pull it out phosphorescent from the endless depths of the unconsciousness, till she was weary, aching, exhausted, and fit to break, and yet she had not done.

Gudrun suffers intensely from her tyrannical mind that exacts the penance of overconsciousness. Her darkness-excluding ego, imprisoning her within a relentless self-awareness, causes Gudrun's separation from peace, from union, from "lapsing out." Though irrevocably single, she is severely limited, living according to an overactive brain that is eternally tortured by memory and victimized by time. The "glittering rope of knowledge" functions as the moon does in the Ursula/Skrebensky consummation scenes: a bitter refulgence, it is a sign of the woman's egoistical isolation.

The lovemaking sequence in "Death and Love" forcefully demonstrates the distinction between Gerald's unfinished self on the one hand, and Gudrun's distorted being on the other. This distinction is inherent in the respective faculties they live by. The will is a dependent faculty of the personality (the central point bears repeating) because it always needs immediate, direct objects on which to exercise itself. Whether venting his rage on the exterior world, or turning desperately to a woman for protection (paradoxically, self-diminishment in womb-like embrace is his defense against complete disintegration), Gerald is emotionally, sometimes passionately, reliant upon something external and *other*. Gudrun, functioning through her abstracting mind, is integral and isolate. Though she suffers from her self-enclosing mind, she is also defended by it, and saved from the humiliating compulsions that strip Gerald of his self-possession. Gerald's interfering will impels him toward the outside world and constantly tears at the boundaries of his self. But living within her consciousness leads Gudrun to a full, frigid independence from other people—though not from the endless "automatic" activity of her mind.

This frigidity is complexly developed and symbolized in two late chapters of the novel, "Continental" and "Snowed Up." Snow provides the setting for the late sections of *Women in Love* and is the last of the novel's major carbon-symbols. But the image does more than indicate that a loveless, abstract quest for sensation has reduced Gudrun and Gerald in a snowy dissolution. The problem with such a reading is that it sees Gerald and Gudrun as equal partners in "ice-destructive knowledge, snow-abstract annihilation." Yet an accurate description of the final stages of their relationship is: Gudrun's lust for "ice-destructive knowledge" causes Gerald's "snow-abstract annihilation." He dies and she lives as she is transformed into a sinister force that destroys him. Her cold-bloodedness becomes so chilling and complete that her soul is fairly imaged by the surrounding snow. Gerald's being, if cold and dehumanized, cannot be identified with the snow in the end: observing the last acts of the two characters, it seems more adequate to say that he is sacrificed to the frozen element within her. For Gerald begins to show positive emotions and become something more than a man of dark rage and will. But Gudrun deliberately goads him, wanting him to remain ungoverned and negative, preventing their connection from taking a creative form and developing wholeness: " 'Won't you say you'll love me always?' she coaxed. . . . 'I will love you always,' he repeated, in real agony, forcing the words out. . . . 'Try to love me a little more, and to want me a little less,' she said, in a half contemptuous, half coaxing tone. The darkness seemed to be swaying in waves across his mind, great waves of darkness plunging across the mind. It seemed to him he was degraded at the very quick, made of no account." Gerald's acknowledged vulnerability, so incongruous in their relationship based on malice, causes his "agony"; and it is her jeering that reduces him to a chaos he no longer wants. Moments like this one help generate the sympathy that many readers feel toward Gerald.

Understanding the relationship of Gerald to the snow, then, is hardly a simple matter; indeed the connection between character and symbol is extremely subtle. Making no pretence at a full elucidation of the startling effects Lawrence achieves through his snow-symbolism, I would point out first that the snow represents a phase in the development of Lawrence's water-imagery. As a literal medium of engulf-ment, water becomes symbolic of the outer world that threatens to figuratively engulf men of unformed ego. In addition the engulfing element indicates the *nature* of the man engulfed; the watery element only drowns a watery man, who lacks solid form. Tom Brangwen is swept away in a flood that represents the death-wish in his unsure being. The brilliant touch of turning the water to snow refers to the mechanistic coldness of Gerald: the frigidity Gerald achieves at his worst is something foreign to Tom. But we have seen that Gerald is not merely mechanistic. The snow tells us at least as much about Gudrun as it does about Gerald. Gerald has a tendency to regress to infantile, dependent states, and his engulfment suggests a reversion to the security of the womb. The snow thus becomes a cruelly ironic but suitable image for Gudrun, the wintry woman Gerald has paradoxi-cally chosen as the object of his reversion.

It is not surprising that high in the Alps Gudrun views a "great cul-de-sac of snow and mountain peaks" that fills her with "strange rapture"; the white enclosure has an enveloping, containing quality: "the cradle of snow ran on the eternal closing-in. . . . This was the centre, the knot, the navel of the world." The dazzled ecstasy Gudrun feels toward the cul-de-sac is aroused because the snow-wound is felt as a contiguous extension of herself. When the snow allows Gudrun a rare moment of self-transcendence, the mystical union places her: Gudrun is revealed as an instance of the principle of universal cold: "If she could but come there, alone, and pass into the infolded navel of eternal snow and of uprising, immortal peaks of snow and rock, she would be a oneness with all, she would be herself the eternal, infinite silence, the sleeping, timeless, frozen centre of the All." Her loss of self is based on discovering an element identical with the self.

Like Gerald, Gudrun is not a one-dimensional character. Her coldness is not preordained, but chosen. Capable of intense, emotional moments, she works to extirpate them. She wills to freeze and numb herself because she sees feeling as the beginning of self-destruction. The wish to prostrate herself in self-abasement before Gerald reveals her fear and her whirlpool-emotions that suck in the self: "She was aware of his frightening, impending figure standing close behind her, she was aware of his hard, strong, unyielding chest, close upon her back. And she felt she could not bear it any more, in a few minutes she would fall down at his feet, grovelling at his feet, and letting him destroy her." The depiction of Gerald's strength demonstrates one reason for Gudrun's frigid egoism, for it shows the immense threat she perceives in his masculinity. She thus finds any momentary loss of control potentially devastating, and must constantly protect herself against her urge for self-prostration before Gerald's power. But above all the problem is in herself. Feeling for her is like a motor that starts a sadomasochistic whirligig, a power struggle she *must* win to survive. The solution is not to feel (Gerald's less effective solution is to vanquish). A thoroughgoing ironic cynicism is her defense against loss of control; the strategy allows her to maintain her cool supremacy and to conquer her masochistic impulses.

Mockery is the mode of Loerke, the German artist Gudrun and Gerald meet during their holiday. Loerke, a pure embodiment of Arctic reduction, is at once protective and stimulating; he denies the natural feelings which, in Gudrun's case, endanger strength, while affirming the mental processes that reinforce her cold integration. Gudrun transfers her favor from Gerald, the master of the machine, to Loerke, the artist of the machine, because of Loerke's disdainfully profound "knowledge in the mystery of dissolution." Gerald spreads disintegration out of uncomprehended drives, but Loerke has an objective understanding of mechanical reduction. Aloof, dispassionate contemplation of cold reducing-down is the most diabolical form of Arctic-being. This is the perverse pleasure Gudrun and Loerke—*not* Gudrun and Gerald—share. Loerke's art interprets the mechanical work, the mechanical play, that he sees as the essence of the contemporary world: "What is man doing when he is at a fair . . .? He is fulfilling the counterpart of labour—the machine works him instead of he the machine. He enjoys the mechanical motion of his own body."

Moreover, he lives this universal principle within his own being. He is himself both mechanical and corruptive; the one develops from the other, for mechanical functioning ends by signifying the corruption of soul and body. Loerke savors the dismemberment of his own ego, the inner corrosion that occurs when the self is frozen shut and unable to love or participate in organic life. Without the growth that comes from creatively natural life, or the hope that derives from belief in a greater ideal, what remains for Loerke is to immerse himself in disintegration, "to explore the sewers [like] the wizard rat that swims ahead." Gudrun, fatigued by Gerald's constant tearing at the borders of the self, desires the processes that take place in the closed envelope of the ego. She accepts the gradual erosion that is inevitable once the ego closes off replenishment and growth from the outside. (Gerald's problem is the reverse, lacking independent integrity his being is exposed to the universe he needs for self-completion; where she is too closed, he is too opened.) Turning now to Loerke, whose mastery of dissolution is supreme, Gudrun devotes herself to "sensation within the ego, the obscene religious mystery of ultimate reduction, the mystic frictional activities of diabolic reducing down, disintegrating the vital organic body of life."

Yet there is a paradox here that critics of *Women in Love* have not noticed. Loerke seduces Gudrun, in fact, with the promise of stability. "[Loerke] was single and, by abstraction from the rest, absolute in himself." The lust for disintegration has an integrating effect. The dismemberment toward which they inexorably move is in the distant future; within the novel, Gudrun and Loerke find a ghastly modus vivendi. If they sometimes experience "inorganic misery," they still do not share Gerald's chaos and doom. It is Gerald, with his trace of human vulnerability and organic feeling, who is destroyed by the death-flow. Unconfused concentration on breaking-down is a way of existence, though it is living for dying.

Gerald increasingly irritates Gudrun as his strenuous will and his insistent, laborious energy interfere with her: "She was weary, oh so weary of Gerald's gripped intensity of physical motion." Gerald intrudes on the exhilarating freedom Gudrun and Loerke find by "rising above" the tedious world, "the dreariness of actuality, the monotony of contingencies." Theirs is a superiority of indifference, a sardonic intactness that comes from conceiving life as pure game. Their play pretends that action has no consequence and exults in cynicism. Without belief in life's positive meaning, there is only disintegration and that is best enjoyed when flavored with mockery. What remains for them is cynical jokes and nihilistic fancies, to play as the world approaches its end. The snow is the ideal backdrop for their inhuman gaity.

In the climactic, final scene between the three characters, Gerald's rigid jealousy suddenly ruins Gudrun and Loerke's "perfect . . . silvery isolation and interplay." Loerke's savoir faire, with its combination of derision and whimsy, continues despite Gerald's determined intrusion on the careless scene; the little artist's contemptuous gallantry drives Gerald to violence. But the blows he gives the smaller, weaker man are paltry compared to the "great downward stroke" Gudrun delivers to Gerald's face and chest. (This is, allegorically, his execution, that "last" blow referred to in "Water-Party.") Gerald responds insanely, seizing Gudrun by the throat; this is an act of the dependent will in extremis;

murder, in Gerald's case, is the most vicious, yet most pathetic, admission of the need to have a profound effect on an object. Through the strangling, Gerald shatters Gudrun's remoteness, and forces from her, at last, a total, passionate reaction: "The struggling was her reciprocal lustful passion in this embrace, the more violent it became, the greater the frenzy of delight, till the zenith was reached, the crisis, the struggle was overborne, her movement became softer, appeased."

Yet he soon abandons the attack, because Gerald is less murderer than self-destroyer. His murderous and suicidal impulses are both rooted in an unsubstantiality of self. Choking Gudrun is a bizarre way to achieve fusion, but he finds a deeper, more satisfying merger by dissolving into the "hollow basin of snow." Gerald fades unconsciously into the snowbanks, losing all life-direction: "He drifted, as on a wind, veered, and went drifting away." When he drifts into nothingness, releasing his grasp on being, as when he attempts murder, driven helplessly to destroy Gudrun's more integral being, Gerald is admitting the defeat of the self.

Disappearing into the snow-basin, Gerald creates a pantomime of his relationship with Gudrun. He literally recapitulates what he has long been undergoing metaphorically: union-in-frigidity, self-reduction in an enclosure that rejects and freezes him. There was always a paradox in Gerald's bringing his merger-need to so chilling a receiver as Gudrun. Why should Gerald look for his intermingling to a woman that rejects him, unless his urge to be saved hides a stronger urge to be destroyed. High in the glacial mountans he resolves the contradiction when he moves toward his death. Gerald dies under a "small bright moon," a "painful brilliant thing" that contributes to the fatigued confusion of his last moments. The image interweaves the death with the larger pattern of Lawrence's symbolic events, for moon suggests Gudrun's unified, malevolently separate ego, and snow its punishing counterpart, the fate that is left to Gerald when he depends on a woman who evades him.

Gerald's death brings together his longing for fusion and his self-destructive impulses: indeed the one is included in the other. Instilling one identity into another is finally impossible, but the desired dissolution of self can be achieved in death. And by immersing himself in the perfect metaphor for her, Gerald simulates the longed-for symbiosis with Gudrun. Blinded by the moonlight he cannot "escape," Gerald moves toward the "hollow basin" of snow; there he stumbles toward a frozen peace in an icy womb.

On the Shape the Self Takes

Baruch Hochman

Lawrence's view of the self, and his way of depicting it, are not homogeneous throughout his career. Nor are his views and his strategies consistent from one phase of his development to another. The large outlines, however, are moderately consistent, and they involve a linking of the natural, the organic, and the spontaneous, as against the social, the mechanical, and the compulsive. Yet even at his most radical, Lawrence does not simply contrast the sets of terms. His view is, with occasional lapses, dialectical and complex. He does not, for example, assume that spontaneity is a natural *given* of experience, so that children or primitives can possess it. Nor does he hold that spontaneity, when achieved, gives its possessors the flexibility and the naturalness Lawrence craves. Quite the contrary. Even in his New Mexico phase, when he plays elaborately with the lure of the primitive—as in *St. Mawr, The Princess*, and *The Woman Who Rode Away*—the primitive turns out to be as brutal and as compulsive as the "God in the machine" that drives the doomed characters in *Women in Love*. What he confronts, in fact, is the impossibility of primitivistic reversion, and the necessity in men for the mediation of nature by culture, and of instinct by consciousness. Consciousness may become the villain, but without consciousness man—at least modern man—is doomed. Rupert Birkin's escape from the sinking ship of civilization may not be wholly convincing, but it reflects Lawrence's belief that without consciousness nothing is possible, and that man must find

From *The Test of Character: From the Victorian Novel to the Modern.* © 1983 by Associated University Presses.

some way of coming into being by consciously yielding himself to the darkness out of which, in his view, identity is born.

All Lawrence's work, it seems to me, is concerned in one way and another with the shape identity takes, and then with the place of consciousness in mediating it. *Women in Love* is perhaps the richest and most fully articulated study of the problem. Indeed, *Women in Love* is the novel in which Lawrence most systematically and programmatically probes the depths of the self, and strives to link depth to surface. In doing so he also implies the relation of past to present, and infant self or need to adult configurations of being, free and unfree. And he moots the question of the shape the self can find, and the nature of that shape when it can be found.

Lawrence's exploration of the issue here, as elsewhere, is embodied in a familiar set of images, clearly the heritage of the Romantic age, which pits the organic against the mechanical, and proliferates images of life and death in terms of this dichotomy. Ursula, the ultimately positive figure in the novel, has golden-green eyes and the light of dawning in her face; Hermione is a priestess figure, obscurely linked to the obscene mysteries of the world of death and the dead; Gerald, for all the clear, arctic light that surrounds him, is the "God in the machine," a figure of massed, mechanical motion. Ursula, Birkin, Hermione, Gerald, and Gudrun are the key figures of Lawrence's exploration, the pairs of couples, crossed the reticulated, that Lawrence, speaking of *The White Peacock*, said was the simplest formula for a novel. Hermione, Gerald, and Gudrun, however, are the effective focus of the novel's exploratory life, since Lawrence takes the trouble to provide all three with vivid, if not equally probing, psychologies, while Birkin and Ursula are handled schematically and unprobingly, largely in terms of images and ideas that are merely counterpointed with the reality of the other three.

In all three negative figures what is most striking is the way their rigid outer form encloses inner chaos, and it is felt to be a reaction to that chaos. The formed, form-imposing, form-seeking self is felt to be not a source of value but a product of terror and dread—of the recoil from threatening modes of death and darkness that inhabit its deepest recesses. One of the novel's central interests, it seems to me, lies in defining the patterns of response to such darkness, and in sketching some way of establishing a self that can integrate it rather than be dominated by it.

The sense of the patterned self as defense against chaos is projected from the outset in the figure of Hermione. We first see her at Laura Crich's wedding, decked out to perfection, and anxiously clenched against the darkness within. "She was impressive," we are told, in her lovely pale-yellow and brownish-rose, yet macabre, something repulsive. People were silent as she passed, impressed, roused, wanting to jeer, yet for some reason silenced. Her long, pale face, that she carried lifted up, somewhat in the Rossetti fashion, seemed almost drugged, *as if a strange mass of thoughts coiled in the darkness within her,* and she was never allowed to escape. (My italics.)

Later in the same scene, we hear that she knew

perfectly that her appearance was complete and perfect, according to the first standards, yet she suffered a torture, under her confidence and her pride, feeling herself exposed to wounds and to mockery and to despite. She always felt vulnerable, vulnerable, there was always a secret chink in her armour. She did not know herself what it was. It was a lack of robust self, she had no natural sufficiency, *there was a terrible void, a lack, a deficiency of being within her.* (My italics.)

She was, we hear, "established on the sand, built over a chasm," so that

all the while the pensive, tortured woman piled up her own *defenses of aesthetic knowledge, and culture, and world-visions, and disinterestedness.* Yet she could never stop up the terrible gap of insufficiency. (My italics.)

The emptiness in Hermione—the "deficiency," the "insufficiency" of being—culminates in her murderous assault on Birkin. It is not quite clear with Hermione, as it is with Gerald, whether the thoughts that are coiled in the darkness of her flawed being are the spawn of her inherent aggressiveness or whether they are a response to her essential sense of impotence, or absence, or emptiness. Many elements in her portrayal would seem to suggest the latter—that the insufficiency springs from a sense of phallic absence. Indeed, it seems to me that, given the emphasis on phallic elements both in her portrayal and that of Gerald, we cannot but assume that Lawrence was working from such an imaginative center. Still, the manifest thrust of the novel as a whole reflects a concern with what recent critics have called the ontological problem in Lawrence, the problem of a character's lack of a sense of thereness, of quiddity, of existence, without any reasoned interest in the Freudian dimension of such a lack. Hermione's clutching at Birkin, like Miriam's clutching at Paul in *Sons and Lovers,* as well as the "weird"-ness of her sybilline, rhapsode's manner, is seen to be a way of containing and controlling the absence that violence inhabits. Like Miriam, Hermione walks with muscle-clenched hips; like Miriam, who breaks the handle off a cup in her trance of taut withdrawal, she is felt to be jammed with violence. Her final desperation, when Birkin eludes her, is seen to be a response to the defection of the one being she felt could fill her void. Lawrence's entire treatment suggests that the violence she directs at Birkin matters more in itself than the question of whether it is the cause or the consequence of her ontological hollow-ness. Whatever its derivation, her homicidal violence comes to be seen as the quintessential expression of herself. Hermione's true shape is the shape, such as it is, of her essential violence, and not of her elegant, eloquently defensive modes of social, cultural, and sartorial self-definition.

The same, ultimately, is felt to be true of Gerald. In Gerald, the dialectic of the massively formed, formally massed surface and the pulpy, chaotic depth is far more dramatic, and points toward a richly intimated field of struggle and experience. It is also more revealing of the underlying logic of the tension, posed as it is in counterpoint to the analogous dialectic of Gudrun's being, which in turn is sharply defined in relation to Ursula's. In counterposition to Gerald, all the characters enter into a structure of analogous actions, defining—within the limits of this novel's possibilities—the issue of self and its modes of articulation.

Granted Lawrence's pervasive concern with the distinction be-tween organism and mechanism, one of the most striking things about the portrayal of Gerald is the general absence within it of simple images of mechanism as such to evoke the workings of his personality, and the defensive function of the surfaces it presents to the world. Al-though he is the "God in the machine," and although we learn that he resorts to the espousal of formal dress as a defense against the anarchy that prevails at Shortlands, only once are we asked to see him (and then through Gudrun's hostile eyes) as we see the little Marchioness at Breadalby, or Winifred's French governess, merely as a beetle, ar-mored. Instead, we are asked to envision him as a hulk of massed energy, congested.

Not surprisingly, this vividly visualized subjugator of a mare (in "Coal Dust") is recurrently envisioned as a stallion, as when, in "Gladiatorial," we hear that "his eyes flared with a sort of terror like the eyes of a stallion," or when he is spoken of as "a dark horse," or—most significantly—when Birkin contemplates him, dead: "But now he was dead, like clay, like bluish, corruptible ice. Birkin looked at the pale fingers, the inert mass. He remembered a dead stallion he had seen: "a dead mass of maleness." As dead matter he has for Birkin "a last terrible look of cold, mute matter." Within Lawrence's conceptual system, such matter is tantamount to chaos, bred in murder.

Within the elaborate bestiary of *Women in Love*, it turns out that the stallion is not chiefly an image of nature or of eros, but rather of compacted rage and terror, of violence that is essentially phallic and batters at women. One expression of this is in the description of Loerke's sculpture, which is of a frail girl riding a "massive, magnificent stallion, rigid with pent-up power. His neck was arched and terrible, like a sickle, its flanks were pressed back, rigid with power." The governing dialectic of the novel links the stallionlike hunk of man (or mass of matter) that is Gerald to the corrosiveness of the violence that fills him.

Altogether, the image system of *Women in Love* points us to a conception—explicit in the novel—of matter itself as formless, unorganized, and destructive. That lack of organization is felt to be the result of inherent violence. The measure of this is the novel's tendency to project the feeling-sense of hostile communication between people as electrical, mesmeric, radiumlike, and so forth. Again and again, revulsion, recoil, and attraction are seen to involve emissions or emanations of buzzing, lethal rays that threaten to shock, poison, or dissolve the object at which they are directed.

The most extreme form of such emanation is probably the literal emission that Gerald discharges into Gudrun, when, in "Death and Love," he immerses himself in her as in "the bath of birth," and discharges all the poisons in his system, "all his pent-up darkness and corrosive death . . . his bitter potion of death." What is involved is the need to purge his system of all the accumulated aggression that has been stirred in the course of his father's dying. Hence the sense, formulated in the account of his response to old Mr. Crich's condition, of the void-that-is-death within him.

> [A]s the fight went on, and all that he had been and was continued to be destroyed, so that life was a hollow shell all round him, roaring and clattering like the sound of the sea . . . he knew he would have to find reinforcements, otherwise he would collapse inward upon the great dark void which circled at the center of his soul. . . . Something must

come up with him into the hollow void of death in his soul,
fill it up, and so equalize the pressure within to the pressure
without. For day by day he felt more and more like a bubble
filled with darkness.

The erotic violence is shown to be the reciprocal of desperate
need, and in a way that specifies the source of the need. In the first
sexual contact between Gerald and Gudrun, Gudrun becomes the
mother of the newborn (or newly reborn) Gerald:

> As he drew nearer to her, he plunged deeper into her envel-
> oping soft warmth, a wonderful creative heat that pene-
> trated his veins and gave him life again. He felt himself
> dissolving and sinking into the bath of her living strength. . . .
> His blood, which seemed to have been drawn back into
> death, came ebbing on the return, surely, beautifully,
> powerfully.
>
> He felt his limbs growing fuller and flexible with life,
> his body gained an unknown strength. He was a man again,
> strong and rounded. And he was a child, so soothed and
> restored and full of gratitude.
>
> And she, she was the great bath of life, he worshipped
> her. Mother and substance of all life she was. And he,
> child and man, received of her and was made whole.
> His pure body was almost killed. But the miraculous, soft
> effluence of her breath suffused over him, over his seared,
> damaged brain, like a healing lymph, like a soft, soothing
> flow of life itself, perfect as if he were bathed in the womb
> again.

Hermione's inner emptiness is a kind of partial blank within the
novel; if we wish, Lawrence makes of it an ontological absolute,
though the text suggests other derivations for it. Gerald's lack, on the
other hand, is elaborately explored in relation to Gudrun, to his mother,
even—at a distance—to his nurse. Indeed, the nurse serves to project a
powerful image of the need that drives Gerald, and to insinuate into
our consciousness an image of him as a furious baby: a baby who in
the rage of his impotence and the impotence of his rage demonically
assaults the world. That image is all the more powerful because we
apprehend it with Gudrun, whose rage at the woman who revels in
having pinched his bottom almost immediately identifies itself as the

reflex of the wish to pinch his bottom herself. Her indignation is a defense against her own wish, her own need.

Yet what Lawrence dramatizes in Gudrun is the way she latches on to Gerald because of her need to identify with the very form she so passionately needs to destroy. That form is shown to be not only Gerald's "natural," physical endowment—the blondness, the arctic aura of ice and snow, the massiveness—but also his own reactive response to his "demonic" destructiveness. Her response to him at first glimpse is a response to his massiveness-cum-separateness.

> [A]bout him was the strange, guarded look, the unconscious glisten, *as if he did not belong to the same creation as the people about him.* Gudrun lighted on him at once. There was something northern about him that magnetized her. In his clear northern flesh and his fair hair was a glisten like sunshine refracted through crystals of ice. And he looked so new, unbroached, pure as an arctic thing. (My italics.)

The same quality grips her in "Diver," as she watches Gerald in the water. There the quality is presented from three vantage points: Gudrun and Ursula's shared one, Gerald's, and Gudrun's alone. As the young women drift along the landscape we see him:

> Suddenly, from the boat-house, a white figure ran out, frightening in its swift sharp transit, across the old landing-stage. It launched in a white arc through the air, there was a bursting of the water, and among the smooth ripples a swimmer was making out to space, in a center of faintly heaving motion. *The whole otherworld, wet and remote,* he had to himself. *He could move into the pure translucency of the grey, uncreated water.* (My italics.)

Then we experience him from what is equivocally the focus of her consciousness, or of his:

> And she stood motionless gazing over the water at the face which washed up and down on the flood, as he swam steadily. *From his separate element* he saw them and he exulted to himself because of his own advantage, his possession of a world to himself. *He was immune and perfect.* (My italics.)

And then we see him solely from Gudrun's vantage point:

> Gudrun envied him almost painfully. Even this momentary
> possession of *pure isolation and fluidity* seemed to her so
> terribly desirable that she felt herself as if damned. . . .
> "God, what it is to be a man!" she cried. (My italics.)

Yet the thing in him that she finds both attractive and enviable—
the thing she in the end compulsively needs to destroy—is directly
linked to the violence she senses in him. It is this violence, the novel
shows us, that determines the shape—the isolated, remote shape—of
his being. In the first scene, following the impression Gudrun takes of
his arctic purity, we hear that "his gleaming beauty, maleness, like a
young, good-humoured, smiling wolf, did not blind her to the significant, sinister stillness in his bearing, the lurking danger of his unsubdued temper. 'His totem is the wolf,' she repeated to herself.' " It
seems no accident that the lurking need for lurking violence leads to
her final alliance with Loerke, who is imaged in terms of free-wheeling
rodentry. Loerke combines childlike qualities with manifest sadism, as
expressed in his relation to the girl who served as the model for the
figure mounted on the stallion in the sculpture mentioned above.

Gudrun herself is seen to be founded on an abyss of insecurity as
to her own identity, an abyss no less profound and no less destructive
than Hermione's. In all the scenes of lovemaking between her and
Gerald, we see her resisting submission to the experience she is undergoing, unable to submerge herself in such darkness that overtakes even
Gerald. Lawrence tells us that instead of lapsing into regenerative
sleep, she lies obsessively awake, uncoiling the snake of memory. In
this as in so much else, Gudrun is dramatically contrasted with Ursula,
who—within the terms of the characteristic Lawrentian ideology—lapses
into darkness, and insists on the irrelevance of her past to her present.
Ursula even insists, in the course of her conflict with her father on the
subject of her marriage, that she is not the daughter of her father, but
of the Holy Ghost.

Indeed, Gudrun's enslavement to memory, and to the dead but
not lost past that it preserves, is contrasted with a single moment of
Ursula's aroused relation to her past, a moment she experiences in the
train, on her way to Innsbruck.

> A few more spectres moving outside on the platform—then
> the bell—then motion again through the level darkness.
> Ursula saw a man with a lantern come out of a farm by the
> railway and cross into the dark farm-buildings. She thought

of the Marsh, the old, intimate farm life at Cossethay. My God, how far she was projected from her childhood, how far she was still to go. In one lifetime one travelled through aeons. The great chasm of memory from her childhood in the intimate country surroundings of Cossethay and the Marsh farm—she remembered the servant Tilly, who used to give her bread and butter sprinkled with brown sugar in the old living-room where the grandfather clock had two pink roses in a basket painted above the figures on the face—and now when she was travelling into the unknown with Birkin, an utter stranger—was so great, that it seemed she had no identity, that the child she had been, playing in Cossethay churchyard, was a little creature of history, not herself.

Later, when "a glimpse of two cattle in their dark stalls . . . reminded Ursula again of home, of the Marsh, of her childhood," she thinks: "Oh, God, could one bear it, this past which had gone down the abyss? Could she bear it, that it had ever been?"

Ursula is separate from her past, but cannot quite lose it; Gudrun is bound to her past, and cannot quite relate to it. Gudrun's obsessive fishing up of things from her past would seem to be compensation for her lack of organic relation to it. And the suggestion is that, as with Gerald, the determining experience of both present and past is violence and destructiveness. The leitmotif of her relation to Gerald is violence: of knives and whetstones, of the crackle of electricity and the shooting of guns. Even the crackle of the starched sheets in her bed, when Gerald first comes to her, suggests the sound of pistol shots. Gudrun has no homicide in her background, as Gerald does; she is no female Cain. But her affinity with Gerald is shown to be an affinity between antagonistic but complementary violences that allure each other, negate each other, neutralize each other. The decisive suggestion is that the apparent completeness and formedness of both Gerald and Gudrun are a reaction formation to the still inchoate chaos at the core of their being.

Sadomasochistic bondage to violence is explicit in the relationship, and—independently—in the makeup of both its partners. Of Gerald's response to Minette, for example, we are told that "the sensation of her inchoate suffering roused the old sharp flame in him, a mordant pity, a passion almost of cruelty." "Rabbit" dramatizes—as do half a dozen other scenes—the searing blood-lust that fixes them to each other. The "mordant" in the Minette passage must be taken literally. This man, who experiences the flesh of women as a tearing of silk, bites that which rends him even as he himself rends.

What is interesting in all this, from my point of view here, is the way that entire pattern of reciprocal violence is related to the matter of form. Mr. Crich's self is seen to derive its shape in the end solely from the will he tenses and clenches against death. Hermione's self is seen to be composed to the end of masking and containing the hollowness at her core and the snake of murder coiled there. Gerald's self is seen as a bubble floating on darkness. It is an isolated, remote, untouchable entity, whose brittleness is the cause of its bubblelike fragility. And Gudrun's self is identified with the miniaturizing form she imposes on the living things she sculpts—and with the get-ups in which she sheathes herself so vividly.

Indeed, one of the more striking aesthetic effects of the novel as a whole is that of the two sisters, Ursula and Gudrun, walking with art nouveau elegance in a variety of landscapes. No reader of the novel can fail to note Lawrence's near-obsession with the colors and combinations of their garments, and this reader has often taken the meticulous specification and iteration of costumes to be a piece of deflected feminine identification—something not wholly surprising in a novel so rich in homosexual impulses. Whatever the source of the preoccupation, however, there is a clear thematic function filled by the feminine habiliments. One of the novel's more vivid effects is that of birdlike, shadelike figures, metallic in their burnishing, that flit through its landscapes, industrial and natural, flitting almost like the figures on the burning pavements of Yeats's "Byzantium." The world of the novel is a kind of hell, and the characters in it present the surfaces of their social selves like both brittle and insect-crusts and evanescent shadows. The women, who suffer the greatest and most manifest vulnerability of all—and the charade of Ruth and Naomi that Ursula and Gudrun enact at Breadalby, miming the soft need and susceptibility of women of and to each other, dramatizes this boldly—are perhaps the most preening, most peacocklike. Their preening would seem to shield the terrified vulnerability that quivers at their core.

The contrast between Ursula and Gudrun dramatizes this terror. Both women are gloved and sheathed in self-consciously gorgeous clothes, but whereas Gudrun, even in bed, never presents any other physical aspect, Ursula is figured forth in terms of a whole panoply of characteristic images, of dawn, of dusky light, of flowers. Ursula too is not envisioned in her physical nakedness; women rarely are in Lawrence. But a set of natural, organic, implicitly fleshly images accompanies her throughout, as though to validate the sense of a spontaneous, natural self, capable of growth and development. In the arcane language of "The Crown" essays, as well as the studies of the unconscious—more or less contemporary with the various drafts of *Women in Love*—Ursula is conceived in terms of metabolism, not catabolism: in terms of life-process, not death-process.

The underlying structure of images is, if we wish, roughly analogous to the structure of images in *Wuthering Heights*. There too we have the counterposition of images of trees, foliage, flowers, fruit that are associated with growth, and images of fixedness and violence, no less natural than the first set, but bearing the opposite significance. The latter images include the furze and whinstone that are associated with Heathcliff. These, in turn, are linked both to Nelly's imaging of him as the coal that lies beneath the heath, and Catherine's sense of him as the eternal rocks beneath. The violence in *Wuthering Heights* has, in a manner of speaking—a manner that, again, I borrow from Dorothy [Van] Ghent—to do with the atom-smashing of rocks, and the given world of cultivated nature. In *Wuthering Heights* that violence arises from the rending of the psyche, and its inability to integrate the dimensions of its primordial needs and desires. There, as here, there is an ambivalent identification with these energies that blast all forms of the known and conceivable self.

Lawrence, to be sure, is not nearly so extreme as Emily Brontë in his capacity to envision and affirm the destructive energies. His attitude to Brontë, and to her relation to the destructive element, was directly expressed when he described her work as involving "agonies and ecstacies of love, and nothing but . . . death . . . death . . . death." He himself, while he vividly evokes the deathly, or catabolic, aspect of experience, is compulsively impelled to affirm some sense of an emergent self that might renew the world. Indeed, the entire imagery of flower and dawn that accompanies Ursula seems meant to signify this: the birth, or emergence, of a natural self that grows through consciousness and beyond it, and that has the palpitating freshness and newness of the glorious world man has violated. The problem of *Women in Love* is that Lawrence does not begin to intimate the sources of the natural, integral self, or the modes of its configuration. His evocation of it is almost wholly through imagery, and it is essentially magical. Such evocation circumvents the critical issue of aggression in Birkin and Ursula, who bespeak the new possibilities of selfhood.

One might suggest, somewhat subversively, that the modalities of aggression in the positive couple are channeled into ideology on the one hand—especially into Birkin's Sunday-school preacher's cant and rant—and into the obscure "rivers of darkness" into which Ursula and Birkin drift. I refer to the rivers of darkness that would seem to have their source in the dark fountains Ursula finds at the base of Birkin's spine, and the sources of darkness he probes in her. Lawrence designates the anal interplay in which they presumably indulge as positive, as one of the ways they move into "being." It is as though some of the classic modes of "Yahoo-ery" are here diverted into the modes of erotic self-expression, into a limited, sanctioned form of polymorphous perversity. Lawrence would seem to subscribe to Birkin's feeling that such rivers are fountains of corruption, but the corruption in their case, unlike that of Loerke, the sewer rat, is felt to be positive. By descending into them, Ursula and Birkin are purified. To use a recurrent Lawrentian metaphor, they undergo a baptism into life, into being, into the purity of fresh flowers and new light, starry and otherwise.

Why this is so is not quite clear. What is clear is that Lawrence, in this doomsday book of his, is for once clearly separating the sheep from the goats, and consigning the one lot to heaven, a heaven of potential flowering, and the other lot to hell, a hell that is at once a condition of metallic harshness and mudlike formlessness. Both the blessed and the damned, however, are beset by the terror, and also the incipient violence, of the absolutely vulnerable. Linking both pairs of lovers is the pain of being touched, of the disintegration that, as Lawrence imagines it, may overtake an individual when he is touched at the quick. All Birkin's talk about the horror of meeting and mingling in love reflects this; so does Ursula's wish to withdraw into the limbo of absolute isolation. Both Gerald and Gudrun cling to each other and withdraw from each other in a frenzy of dread. They fear being touched in the one case, and being pierced to the quick in the other. At the same time the terror of contact is dramatized in terms of its reciprocal, the terror of isolation, in stony coldness, such as Gudrun experiences with Gerald toward the end of the novel. To approach the love-object is to stand in danger of fusing with it. To withdraw from it is to be threatened by utter freeze-out by death in an emotional waste of ice and snow.

In tracing out this pattern, Lawrence, for all the vast distance that separates him from James, is taking up a theme that—as I note [elsewhere]— James, like other nineteenth-century writers, inherited from the tradition of the novel. I mean the theme of entrapment and isolation (not to speak of petrifaction and frigid congealment) within the self, and of the need to break out of that entrapment into contact with others on personal, moral, or social grounds. Lawrence is more than ordinarily obsessed with the issue. It is no surprise that he should be, living as closely as he does to his Protestant, Dissenting origins, and to the promises of fulfillment in selfhood that he grew up into. "The Man Who Loved Islands" is a twentieth-century "Alastor," without the possibility of redemption. And the treatises on psychoanalysis, together with all the rest of the ideological writings, are ranting sermons on the issue of self and society. They center on what is, for Lawrence, the virtually unresolvable conflict between the need to be separate and the need to belong, between the need to be totally self-determining and the need to submerge oneself in others.

"The Trembling Instability" of *Women in Love*

Philip M. Weinstein

Women in Love has elicited more and better criticism than anything else Lawrence wrote. It remains difficult, however, for the commentator faced with "the trembling instability of [its] balance" to refrain from "put[ting] his thumb in the scale, to pull down the balance to his own predilection" ("Morality in the Novel"). In stressing that balance this chapter attends to the novel's textural variety by exploring three different "arenas" of narrative, each concerned with the tension between a set of given cultural arrangements, on the one hand, and a cluster of latent natural impulses, on the other. The first (and the most assured) "arena" is Lawrence's dramatization of what he calls in "The Crown" and "flux of corruption," the destructive rituals of thinking, feeling, and acting that beset society as a whole, and Gerald and Gudrun in particular. The assurance of chapters like "Rabbit," "Death and Love," and "Snowed Up" contrasts markedly with the ambiguities that appear in the second "arena": the Gerald-Birkin relationship. That male pairing, on closer scrutiny, verges on incoherence. It is easy to identify (if not to articulate) the sinister dynamic of the scene with Bismarck: the "gleaming" Gerald beating the rabbit on the neck, Winifred crooning, Gudrun revealed, "her voice like a seagull's cry." By contrast, when Birkin, "with dark, almost vengeful eyes," says to Ursula of the dead Gerald, "He should have loved me, I offered him," his comment is articulate and yet, on reflection, far from clear. Would the offered love have saved Gerald? Was the love offered? What kind of love is in

From *The Semantics of Desire: Changing Models of Identity from Dickens to Joyce.* © 1984 by Princeton University Press. Princeton University Press, 1984.

question? Finally, between these "arenas" of assured critique, on the one hand, and ambiguity or incoherence, on the other, there is the "arena" of Birkin's relationship with Ursula. In my reading of the novel, the rhythm of this relationship best embodies the "trembling instability of the balance" that is *Women in Love*'s finest achievement. Its unpredictable turns lie midway between the clarity of the "flux of corruption" and the confusion of *Blutbrüderschaft*.

"We roam in the belly of our era" ("The Crown"), and "Creme de Menthe" is one of the chapters in *Women in Love* that best display the era's belly. London Bohemia, with its "very thorough rejectors of the world," frequents the Café Pompadour; and though these avant-gardists seek to be free of convention; they remain, as Birkin tells Gerald, "for all their shockingness, all on one note." Their repudiation of respectability has not brought freedom but merely exchanged one social code for another; Lawrence finely conveys the fixed, foreclosed quality of their motions.

Minette's affected lisp, Halliday's self-conscious histrionics—playing up to an audience attuned to his gestures—the protocol of eating and drinking ("But you can't eat oysters when you're drinking brandy," Halliday squeals): programmed moves like these fill the scene as its tension builds. Gerald is instantly placed—by Minette, by Halliday, by the crowd—as Minette's potential lover, and this easy identification stimulates in Gerald "an awful, enjoyable power over her, an instinctive cherishing very near to cruelty." Halliday thrives on the pain of being ousted, and when he screams on discovering Minette in the Pompadour, "the café looked up like animals when they hear a cry." Swiftly—as though the scene had been rehearsed before—the antagonism mounts. A few drops of brandy in Halliday's face leads to talk of blood and beetles, and then to Minette's knifing the young man's hand. The calculated sex-play and the accumulating brutality are not alternative activities; they are versions of an identical dynamic: the programmatic itching of raw nerves, sensual gratification through self-abuse and the abuse—verbal, physical—of others. Within well-ordered confines the Bohemians at the Pompadour avert the ennui that stalks their life by teasing at, toying in public with, the constitutive elements of their passional life. They know they are alive by the lacerating, self-delighting sensations thus produced.

> Minette looked at him with a slow, slow smile. She was
> very handsome, flushed, and confident in dreadful knowl-

edge. Two little points of light glinted on Gerald's eyes.

"Why do they call you Minette? Because you're like a cat?" he asked her.

"I expect so," she said.

The smile grew more intense on his face.

"You are, rather:—or a young, female panther."

"Oh God, Gerald!" said Birkin, in some disgust.

The opposite of animals, these are humans playing at being animals, looking at their animal motions in mirrors. "In our night-time, there's always the electricity switched on," Birkin had told Ursula, and Minette has taken on a cat's name so as to stimulate half-conscious fantasies of animal passion in her potential lovers. Her sexuality is worked, stroked, advertised. The only spontaneous gesture in the chapter is Birkin's rising up involuntarily in disgust. "You're all right," the Russian tells Gerald: you've met the standards, you can sleep with Minette. The chapter closes, not on the mysterious note of Gerald's sexual entry into Minette's "potent darkness," but on the flatly urbane note of blasé, nihilistic Bohemia: "The men lit another cigarette and talked casually."

Behavior at the Pompadour, for all its surface differences, answers to the same terms with which Birkin assesses the social rounds at Breadalby: "how known it all was, like a game with the figures set out . . . the same figures moving round in one of the innumerable permutations that make up the game." Nothing is more achieved in *Women in Love* than Lawrence's scenes of intercourse among those who have a great need but no capacity for it. The conventions of this dominant background serve to silhouette nicely a relationship which reveals quite other impulses and requires for its interpretation a new vocabulary: the inchoate, abortive love between Gerald and Birkin.

> "You don't believe in having any standard of behaviour at all, do you?" he challenged Birkin, censoriously.
>
> "Standard—no. I hate standards. But they're necessary for the common ruck. Anybody who is anything can just be himself and do as he likes. . . . It's the hardest thing in the world to act spontaneously on one's impulses—and it's the only really gentlemanly thing to do—provided you're fit to do it."
>
> "You don't expect me to take you seriously, do you?" asked Gerald. . . . "You think people should just do as they like."

"I think they always do. But I should like them to like the purely individual thing in themselves, which makes them act in singleness. And they only like to do the collective thing."

"And I," said Gerald grimly, "shouldn't like to be in a world of people who acted individually and spontaneously, as you call it. We should have everybody cutting everybody else's throat in five minutes."

"That means *you* would like to be cutting everybody's throat," said Birkin.

"How does that follow?" asked Gerald crossly.

"No man," said Birkin, "cuts another man's throat unless he wants to cut it, and unless the other man wants it cutting. This is a complete truth. It takes two people to make a murder: a murderer and murderee. And a murderee is a man who is murderable. And a man who is murderable is a man who in a profound if hidden lust desires to be murdered."

"Sometimes you talk pure nonsense," said Gerald.

Birkin's joining of a murderer and a murderee as requisite, each, for the other's fulfillment, goes far—farther than he knows. Immediately it proposes the latent form of Gerald's relationship with Gudrun, with each figure playing both roles. Gudrun's swoon (in "Coal Dust") at the sight of Gerald's spurs coming down on the mare's bleeding flanks is caused by the double identification. She is both mare and rider. As Freud writes in *Three Essays on the Theory of Sexuality*. "A person who feels pleasure in producing pain in someone else in a sexual relationship is also capable of enjoying as pleasure any pain which he may himself derive from sexual relations. A sadist is always at the same time a masochist."

Gudrun repudiates any acknowledgment of double roles. When she later rejects Birkin's formulation by calling Gerald's killing his brother "the purest form of accident," she is reserving for herself the right to "accidental" murder.

The Cain reference resonates throughout the narrative. The only major figure with a past that ultimately controls him, Gerald-as-child-murderer is the foremost exception to Lawrence's usually optimistic mode of conceiving the characters he cares for as free to become who they are. Gerald's culture has him by the throat. A useless class-molded education, a pair of frustrated and inescapable parents, lengthy immersion in a brutal and brutalizing profession: in Gerald we measure (as we will later measure it in Clifford Chatterley) the weight of cultural determinants which Lawrence must suspend if he is to free his protagonists to center on their native resources. Birkin (and later Mellors) is revealingly exempted from much of this sinister context, and one reason for Birkin's appealing mobility is his lack of the usual cultural baggage. Gerald is exempted from nothing. His movements in the present are as keyed, Conrad-like, to the fatal accumulation of his past as they are to the unfolding of any future. Joyce Carol Oates has rightly termed him "Lawrence's only tragic figure." He gives the lie to Lawrence's confident assertion that "tragedy is lack of experience." When in "Water-Party" he lets go "for the first time in his life . . . imperceptibly . . . melting into oneness with the whole," the death that is in him—not his life potential—emerges. As David Cavitch has noted, his is the most moving death in Lawrence's work. This is so because Birkin is complicit in that death in ways never acknowledged. "It takes two people to make a murder." It is a relational act, and Birkin is only less implicated than Gudrun. On the page following the conversation already quoted between Gerald and Birkin we read:

> There was a pause of strange enmity between the two men, that was very near to love. It was always the same between them; always their talk brought them into a deadly nearness of contact, a strange, perilous intimacy which was either hate or love, or both. They parted with apparent unconcern, as if their going apart were a trivial occurrence. . . . Yet the heart of each burned from the other. . . . This they would never admit.

How different that earlier interchange looks after this paragraph. The subtext rises into place, and now we really do know that "it's the hardest thing in the world to act spontaneously on one's impulses." What appeared as detached argument is reseen to be relational drama. The Bohemians at the Pompadour were incapable of spontaneous candor and so—despite his argument, *during* his argument—is Rupert Birkin. He too, in his sexual orientation, cannot get clear of "the collective thing." Tugging against the novel's overt commitment to Gerald's death—a murder waiting in the wings, "collectively" in-scribed in both men's inability to transcend their culture's social/sexual mores—is the unexpressed, incompletely expressible cluster of inchoate feelings that they nevertheless bear for each other. Their relationship comes into focus as a tension between the tragic conclusion premised in the Cain symbolism and the whispered possibility, despite Cain, of *Blutbrüderschaft* that is intimated in their cryptic looks and gestures.

Frank Kermode has persuasively claimed that the most important point to note about the prologue to *Women in Love* is that Lawrence struck it out, thus preserving the indecisiveness of his novel's treatment of male love. Whereas the unpublished prologue centers almost feverishly on Birkin's unuttered feelings, the novel itself dramatizes the quandary of male love as the joint concern of both men. A private feeling has been transformed into an abortive relationship, and the moral interest of that relationship inheres in Lawrence's inability to expose its felt life to full conceptualization or assessment. Beneath the overt drama of focused ideas we find the latent drama of undelivered feelings. *Women in Love* is most provocative as a novel of ideas in just the measure that its proclaimed ideas are affected by the cluster of unarticulated feelings they emerge from and descend into.

Consider the scene between the two men "In the Train." Birkin espouses there his doctrine of "the finality of love" with a woman: perfect marriage. If we read the scene dramatically, we find, beneath the clear doctrinal positions, an ambivalent dance of feelings between the two men. Birkin concedes, under its spell, his occasional hatred—his starry hatred—of Gerald; they watch each other warily. Gerald's questions about love elicit Birkin's claim that "I do—I want to love," but to Gerald's ears "it sounded as if he were insistent rather than confident." Gerald continues quietly to mock Birkin's now rather strident claim, and "Birkin could not help seeing how beautiful and soldierly [Gerald's] face was, with a certain courage to be indifferent." Birkin grows angry, "You are a born unbeliever," but Gerald responds: "I only feel what I feel."

> And he looked again at Birkin almost sardonically, with his blue, manly, sharp-lighted eyes. Birkin's eyes were at the moment full of anger. But swiftly they became troubled, doubtful, then full of a warm, rich affectionateness and laughter.
>
> "It troubles me very much, Gerald," he said, wrinkling his brows.
>
> "I can see it does," said Gerald uncovering his mouth in a manly, quick, soldierly laugh.

The scene continues in another mode, one of narrative conceptualization, and now begins to stress (at Gerald's expense) the differences between the two men. "There was something very congenial to him in Birkin. But yet, beyond this, he did not take much notice. He felt that he, himself, Gerald, had harder and more durable truths than any the other man knew." Responding to the tension between the scene's two modes of discourse, we see that Birkin is not merely stating his views; he is trying to believe them. Gerald's finer "manly" candor, his "soldierly" willingness actually to "feel what I feel," momentarily emerges in the dialogue as its center, as the unstated challenge (felt by Birkin as well) to Birkin's doctrinal position. But it quickly disappears in the conceptual prose that reminds us of Gerald's conventionality. Most critics take the reminder so well to heart that they forget the candor of Gerald that had preceded it.

Two longish bedroom scenes—that they take place in bedrooms is not irrelevant—occur before the decisive wrestling match. In the first, at Breadalby, Gerald is trying to sort out his mix of feelings toward Minette. He remains in Birkin's room despite the latter's urging him to go to bed. Birkin eventually wearies of the Minette issue, and Gerald says, " 'I wish you'd tell me something that *did* matter,' looking down all the time at the face of the other man, waiting for something." Nothing comes, Gerald retires, and the next morning as soon as he awakens he recommences the conversation:

> "What am I to do at all, then?" came Gerald's voice.
> "What you like. What am I to do myself?"
> In the silence Birkin could feel Gerald musing this fact.
> "I'm blest if I know," came the good-humoured answer.
> "You see," said Birkin, "part of you wants Minette, and nothing but Minette, part of you wants the mines, the business, and nothing but the business—and there you are— all in bits—"
> "And part of me wants something else," said Gerald, in a queer, quiet, real voice.
> "What?" said Birkin, rather surprised.
> "That's what I hoped you could tell me," said Gerald.

The interchange contains a plea for recognition and intimacy. Gerald cannot identify his own feelings, and Birkin seems incapable of doing it for him. The grooved round of rituals at Breadalby further discourages discovery; the two men move their separate ways.

Later, during Birkin's illness after the "Water-Party" disaster, Gerald visits him in his rooms. The scene is intense; they discuss Gerald's contretemps with Gudrun, and Birkin's conviction that "there's a long way to go, after the point of intrinsic death, before we disappear." Birkin urges Gerald to "keep entirely out of the line. It's no good trying to toe the line, when your one impulse is to smash up the line." The scene thus establishes Birkin as seeking to act on his unconscious impulses, while Gerald remains defensive and afraid to break out of his sterile patterns. In this posture Birkin recognizes most fully his love for Gerald—"of course he had been loving Gerald all along, and all along denying it"—and he rises for the first time into utterance, proposing his pact of *Blutbrüderschaft*. Gerald is tempted but reserved; he backs off: "We'll leave it till I understand it better." Birkin then reaches his often quoted assessment of Gerald: "This strange sense of fatality in Gerald, as if he were limited to one form of existence, one knowledge, one activity, a sort of fatal halfness, which to himself seemed wholeness . . . Gerald could never fly away from himself, in real indifferent gaiety." Discussion of the scene usually ends here, each figure in his characteristic stance of openness and closure, but the conclusion three pages later deserves notice:

> Gerald came near the bed and stood looking down at Birkin whose throat was exposed, whose tossed hair fell attractively on the warm brow, above the eyes that were so unchallenged and still in the satirical face. Gerald, full-limbed and turgid with energy, stood unwilling to go. . . .
>
> "So," said Birkin. "Good-bye." And he reached out his hand from under the bed-clothes, smiling with a glimmering look. . . .
>
> The eyes of the two men met again. Gerald's . . . were suffused now with warm light and with unadmitted love, Birkin looked back as out of a darkness, unsounded and unknown, yet with a kind of warmth, that seemed to flow over Gerald's brain like a fertile sleep.
>
> "Good-bye, then" [Gerald says]. "There's nothing I can do for you?"
>
> "Nothing, thanks."

To take this passage into account is to see that Gerald is not simply the denier. He has verbally retreated but physically advanced, and his "unadmitted love" emerges in his lingering over Birkin and asking if he can do anything. "Nothing," Birkin replies, and at the least the roles of initiation and recoil shift here, complicating our response to both men.

The wrestling scene crystallizes their mutual attraction. It is one of the supreme things in Lawrence, and it eludes the extremes of commentary that would find in it either the clear superiority of homosexual desire or merely (in Mark Spilka's phrase) the working through of Birkin's desire for Gerald "before he can love Ursula 'body and soul' " ("Lawrence Up-Tight"). It neither gives the lie to heterosexual love nor acts as an impediment to heterosexual love that must be worked through and beyond. Rather, the wrestling scene is Lawrence's fullest expression of carnal desire between males, only thinly displaced as wrestling, and yet inadmissible without that displacement. What the men feel for each other is simultaneously precious and unacceptable; no one can read the scene without sensing its cathartic release of tensions. As though magically freed of his fear of sexual fusion, Birkin penetrates deeper and deeper into Gerald, the mind lapsed out, "there was no head to be seen, only the swift, tight limbs, the solid white backs, the physical junction of two bodies clinched into oneness."

Trouble returns with consciousness, for Lawrence can endow neither man with categories that accept these feelings undisplaced. "One ought to wrestle and strive and be physically close. It makes one sane," Birkin asserts. "We are mentally, spiritually intimate, therefore we should be more or less physically intimate too—it is more whole," he repeats. "I don't know why one should have to justify oneself," he states a moment later. "One should enjoy what is given. . . . We should enjoy everything." Birkin may not know why justification is required, but he manifestly requires it. His compulsive "shoulds" and his self-evasive recourse to the pronoun "one" betoken a mind seeking to overcome internal resistance, to combat the strictures of returning consciousness. Gerald, significantly, says little after the wrestling. He has had his intimacy with Birkin, mindlessly; he will never get further in the head. The chapter ends with Gerald glimpsing that he is, indeed, played out: "And mind you, I don't care how it is with me—I don't care how it is—so long as I don't feel . . . so long as I feel I've *lived*, somehow." Almost retrospectively, Gerald surveys his life from its imagined and inevitable terminal point.

Only once more, on the edge of a marriage decision for himself, does Gerald importune Birkin as we have seen in the preceding encounters. Birkin is about to marry, and a quietly desperate Gerald says:

> "One comes to the point where one must take a step in
> one direction or another. And marriage is one direction—"
> "And what is the other?" asked Birkin quickly.
> Gerald looked up at him with hot, strangely-conscious
> eyes, that the other man could not understand.
> "I can't say," he replied. "If I knew *that*—" He moved
> uneasily on his feet and did not finish.
> "You mean if you knew the alternative?" asked Birkin.
> "And since you don't know it, marriage is a *pis aller*."
> Gerald looked up at Birkin with the same hot, constrained
> eyes.

Lawrence will not say either, and we are left to register for ourselves
the meaning of those "hot, strangely-conscious eyes." The scene is
deliberately cryptic; Gerald cannot verbalize what he wants from Birkin.
The point is that it is Gerald who wants something, Gerald the suppli-
ant, and that the novel refuses to assess, even to identify, what he
desires.

At the end of "Continental," the half-crazed Gerald listens to
Birkin's bitter reminder: " 'I've loved you, as well as Gudrun, don't
forget.' 'Have you?' [Gerald] said, with icy skepticism. 'Or do you
think you have?' He was hardly responsible for what he said." Who-
ever is responsible, the words reverberate. It takes two men to make a
murder, two men to produce a failed relationship. "He should have
loved me, I offered him," Birkin tearfully addresses Ursula, in the
presence of Gerald's frozen carcass. The tears bespeak an unacknowl-
edged rejection lurking beneath that offer, a relationship whose failure
goes deeper than any of the novel's conceptual explanations can explain. "When these feeling-patterns become inadequate . . . we are in
torture," Lawrence had written in "The Good Man." "Something is
inadequate in the expressive-apparatus, and we hear strange howlings." In the relationship of Gerald and Birkin, if we listen closely, we
hear such howlings.

> "It is true what I say; there is a beyond, in you, in me,
> which is further than love, beyond the scope, as stars are
> beyond the scope of vision, some of them."
> "Then there is no love," cried Ursula.
> "Ultimately, no, there is something else. But, ultimately,
> there *is* no love."
> Ursula was given over to this statement for some mo-

ments, then she half rose from her chair, saying, in a final, repellant voice:

"Then let me go home—what am I doing here?"

"There is the door," he said. "You are a free agent."

He was suspended finely and perfectly in this extremity. She hung motionless for some seconds, then she sat down again.

"If there is no love, what is there?" she cried, almost jeering.

This sequence takes place in "Mino," and it admirably captures the rhythm of the Ursula-Birkin relationship. Neither perfectly resolved at the conceptual level nor verging on incoherence beneath the argument, the passage from "Mino" shows Birkin and Ursula at a stalemate—and at the same time weathering that stalemate. Ursula repudiates her lover's arguments, even as her motions and his bear out the point he would articulate: "He was suspended finely. . . . She hung motionless . . . then she sat down again." She stays to argue, but surely the important thing is that she stays. Bonded as though gravitationally, held together by what each of them intrinsically is, Ursula and Birkin argue incessantly in *Women in Love*. Argument is for them, as it seems to have been for Frieda and Lawrence, the enduring form of their bond.

Critics tend to disparage "Mino." Especially they lament the failure of its symbolism. H. M. Daleski is representative in conceding "the sad truth . . . that the 'wild cat' is very easily tamed," and C. Pirenet dismisses the chapter from serious concern: "tour ceci est du domaine de la comédie." We *are* dealing with comedy in "Mino": the deepest rhythm of the Birkin-Ursula relationship, symbolism and gesture, argument and embrace, is a comic rhythm. The gap between the Mino's actual behavior and Birkin's assertion of cosmic meanings is not a sign of novelistic failure but the enabling point of contention that fills the chapter. Birkin presses for a will to power, but Ursula is not having any. "There you are—a star in its orbit! A satellite—a satellite of Mars—that's what she is to be! There—there—you've given yourself away! You want a satellite. . . . You've said it—you've said it—you've dished yourself!"

Birkin may be "dished" for argument (though he never *said* "satellite"), but he is anything but rebuffed as a lover. "He stood smiling in frustration and amusement and irritation and admiration and love.

She was so quick, and so lambent, like discernible fire, and so vindictive, and so rich in her dangerous flamy sensitiveness." These are not the thoughts of a disappointed man. The chapter reveals a supple dialectic between argument and feeling, each unpredictably inflecting the other. They fight, they mock, they subside in tenderness, they flare up in passion or in anger, they fight again.

> "But don't you think me good-looking?" she persisted in
> a mocking voice.
> He looked at her, to see if he felt that she was good-looking.

A smile is as appropriate a critical response to this passage as a knowing frown. What Birkin wants is unutterable because he has never experienced it: the perfect release, through their unconventional bond, of their unconventional selves. "It is quite inhuman—so there can be no calling to book, in any form whatsoever—because one is outside the pale of all that is accepted, and nothing known applies." A miracle of spontaneous good form is what he seeks, yet Ursula is no fool for not following his desire immediately. Within the dramatized scene, Birkin's argument for freedom appears as an expression of domination; his insistence on the stars, an evasion of the body. (After the encounter with Hermione one understands why he fights shy.) Ursula mocks him, he takes it for a while and then retreats into his dignity:

> "All right," he said, looking up with sudden exasperation. "Now go away then, and leave me alone. I don't want any more of your meretricious persiflage."
> "Is it really persiflage?" she mocked, her face really relaxing into laughter. She interpreted it, that he had made a deep confession of love to her. But he was so absurd in his words, also.
> They were silent for many minutes, she was pleased and elated like [a] child. His concentration broke, he began to look at her simply and naturally.
> "What I want is a strange conjunction with you."

Lawrence captures "the trembling instability" of their living relationship: his huffiness, her softening, her conviction (half-true, half-false) that he has confessed his love, his easing into intimacy, and then, refreshed, his launching into further argument. He introduces the stars. "Isn't this rather sudden?" she mocks, he laughs, and the two cats take over the scene. Nothing has been resolved, and the symbolic cats only accentuate their disagreement. The landlady enters to announce that tea is ready, their internal chemistry begins to alter, and in the midst of further bickering Ursula breaks out with "What *good* things to eat!" "Take your own sugar," he answers her.

Only an ideologue would want this changed. Lawrence is one of the few novelists (Joyce is another) to render arguing and eating as dissimilar but related activities performed by the same living subject. What is unresolved in argument is mercifully overlooked, forgotten, while eating. They soon begin to argue again, each pressing for his own version of the coming relationship. Eventually, "they had talked and struggled till they were both wearied out."

> "Tell me about yourself and your people," he said.
> And she told him about the Brangwens, and about her mother, and about Skrebensky, her first love, and about her later experiences. He sat very still, watching her as she talked. And he seemed to listen with reverence. Her face was beautiful and full of baffled light as she told him all the things that had hurt her or perplexed her so deeply. He seemed to warm and comfort his soul at the beautiful light of her nature.

Their differences are not superficial, but what joins them is deeper: they are already releasing each other, unconsciously, during those intervals when they forget to maintain their self-defining attributes, when they just let themselves be. The argument, they know, cannot be won by either. "But I want us to be together without bothering about ourselves—to be really together because we *are* together, as if it were a phenomenon, not a thing we have to maintain by our own effort," Birkin urges in "Moony." Irresistible as this is, Ursula resists it —"No, you are just egocentric," she replies—and in her resistance she reestablishes the rhythm of argument and intimacy that is the unchosen mark of their relationship.

This rhythm of unpredictable flame-life characterizes not only "Mino" but the larger form of *Women in Love* as well. Too often critics analyze individual chapters as static entities and then conclude on the note of stalemate, cosmic despair, or equally cosmic triumph. But flame-life flickers, and the career of the flicker is usually comic. In "Moony" the movement of feeling follows a similar pattern, with kindred implications.

Ursula descends to Willey Water and discovers Birkin cursing "Cybele . . . Syria Dea," while he hurls rocks at the moon's reflection on the water. Rather than offer another interpretation of this over-interpreted symbolic act, I would note that his action exhausts his anger.

> "Why should you hate the moon? It hasn't done you any harm, has it?"
> "Was it hate?" he said.
> And they were silent for a few minutes.

He gradually draws close to her and—in a telling reversal of his former action—he says: "There is a golden light in you, which I wish you would give me." The moon that had oppressed him he now desires; they each quietly reveal their sense of lack. Their lacks, of course, differ, and the scene turns from gentleness to altercation, each insisting that the other yield. They grow peaceful again; he teases her about her war cry and concedes that he loves her.

> "Are you sure?" she said, nestling happily near to him.
> "Quite sure—so now have done—accept it and have done."
> She was nestled quite close to him.
> "Have done with what?" she murmured happily.

Their intimacy increases, and he kisses her with his soft, moth-like kisses. In her difference she is kindled and wants passion. He resists and she goes home. Then, with uncanny rightness, Lawrence registers a return in Birkin's spirit toward her. He visualizes his plight of unrelatedness on a cosmic scale, and he sees that if he does not marry he will die. Filled with a vision of sacred marriage as a state of supremely balanced singleness and connection, pride and submission, he rushes to Beldover. "They must marry at once, and so make a definite pledge, enter into a definite communion. . . . There was no moment to spare."

Lawrence's ability to keep his hand off the scale appears in what follows. Birkin's vision reflects, after all, his desires, not Ursula's nor the disposition of the world outside those desires. Will Brangwen enters the chapter at this point—*the* Lawrentian figure who has failed to center his life on his own desires—and he and Birkin engage in an inconsequent discussion of Ursula's upbringing and Birkin's purposes. Each man rebukes the other by saying that Ursula will please herself, and it is fine that she should, upon her entry into the scene, enrage them both by pleasing herself. They each withdraw, baffled and angry, Ursula joining Gudrun and Birkin finding the consolation of wrestling with Gerald at Shortlands.

After the wrestling scene Ursula begins to regain "ascendance over Birkin's being. . . . Gerald was becoming dim again, lapsing out of him." The final ascendance is realized some fifty pages later in "Excurse," but before attending briefly to that climax I would generalize the pattern I have been following. In the imaginative world of Lawrence one centers on carbon or flame, but one neither wills the shape of one's carbon nor dictates the flow of one's flame. The union of Ursula and Birkin comes when it comes, not when one of them sees fit to make it happen. The movement of the novel from "Moony" through "Gladiatorial" follows the unpredictable career of desire, of developments beyond the aegis of the characters' will. In "Excurse" this rhythm is most pronounced.

Discussion of "Excurse" usually focuses on the climaxes and scants their sustained preparation. Locally the quarrel between the lovers derives from the tea party at Hermione's the day before, with its invidious display of well-bred polylingual culture, in the shadow of which Ursula feels vulgar, dumpy, lower-middle-class. She is sure Birkin's rings will not fit her fat fingers. Beneath the local quarrel is the essential one: the passional differences between them—her wanting to engulf him, his still-lingering, sham-spiritual tie to Hermione—threaten to burst them asunder. The magnificent battle they engage in is, reasonably, followed by their magnificent love-making; no one disputes the dynamic. But whereas their anger is irrefutably alive on the page, critics have been wondering for at least thirty years what is happening in their ecstatic union.

The fight clears the air. Ursula's invective identifies and for the moment dissolves the knot of contradictions Birkin carries within himself.

> He wanted her to come back. He breathed lightly and regularly like an infant, that breathes innocently, beyond the touch of responsibility.
> She was coming back. He saw her drifting desultorily under the high hedge, advancing towards him slowly. He did not move, he did not look again. He was as if asleep, at peace, slumbering and utterly relaxed.

She was coming back. The core of Lawrence's art is in his creative grasp of how we leave and return, how our flame-life flares, gutters, renews itself. There follows the gentlest love scene in Lawrence's work.

> She looked up at him. The wonderful yellow light in her eyes now was soft and yielded. . . . He kissed her softly, many, many times. A laugh came into her eyes.
>
> "Did I abuse you?" she asked.
>
> He smiled too, and took her hand, that was so soft and given.
>
> "Never mind," she said, "it is all for the good." He kissed her again, softly, many times.
>
> "Isn't it?" she said.
>
> "Certainly," he replied. "Wait! I shall have my own back."
>
> She laughed suddenly, with a wild catch in her voice, and flung her arms around him.
>
> "You are mine, my love, aren't you?" she cried, straining him close.
>
> "Yes," he said softly.
>
> His voice was so soft and final, she went very still, as if under a fate which had taken her. Yes, she acquiesced—but it was accomplished without her acquiescence. He was kissing her quietly, repeatedly, with a soft, still happiness that almost made her heart stop beating. . . . She hid her face on his shoulder, hiding before him, because he could see her so completely. She knew he loved her, and she was afraid, she was in a strange element, a new heaven round about her. She wished he was passionate, because in passion she was at home. But this was so still and frail, as space is more frightening than force.

Roger Sale claims, without exaggeration, that "almost a thousand pages [of *The Rainbow* and *Women in Love*] lie behind that 'space is more frightening than force,' and we need almost every one to read it rightly." Space is the peaceful dimension you get to without willing it, once you break away from a self-manipulated identity; force is what that instrumental identity can make happen. The quoted passage is transparent and serene, a moment of the cessation of will and the unsought achievement of intimacy. His soft kisses are now what she wants, his unabrasive closeness is the "new heaven round about her."

There is no need to discuss in any detail the remainder of the chapter. Its passionate climaxes seem, for many reasons, less clear and assured than the scene of rebirth just quoted. In certain places, like "the immemorial magnificence of mystic, palpable, real otherness," the later prose of "Excurse" is positively opaque. Garrett Stewart justifies such prose as "Lawrence's post-orgastic style, the prose not of frictional rush to climax, but of the poise and reciprocal peace that ensues. Otherness must be grammatically respected." Perhaps, but what I hear in that phrasing is neither poise nor grammatical respect, but the insistent alliteration of m's: the language of force asserting a transcendent experience rather than the language of space creating the image of it.

Mystic climaxes are in any case only one part of *Women in Love*. The flame-life does not remain fixed in any supreme ecstasy. The rarer achievement is not some incandescent perfection of Ursula and Birkin's relationship but its mobile, phoenix-like capacity to continue under duress. Beset by Birkin's fear of merging, shadowed by his desire for an "eternal union with a man too," their intimacy is most impressive where least assertive. Not created by argument, it quietly survives the thrust of the closing argument of the novel, as it has survived other arguments. "Anything that *triumphs*, perishes," Lawrence wrote in "The Crown."

At its best, this novel imagines a relationship so open to its own shortcomings and yet surviving by this very openness, that it does elude the finalities of victory or defeat. Gerald and Gudrun ride their aggression and insecurity to death or spiritual disintegration. Gerald and Birkin press each other for an alternative response that neither can articulate. But Birkin and Ursula achieve the "trembling instability of the balance," a living relationship that hurts because of its inadequacy, hurts also because it is alive. The novel that can, among its other achievements, render these three modes of experience as continuous reflections of each other, is rightly seen as Lawrence's masterpiece.

Women in Love:
D. H. Lawrence's Judgment Book

Maria DiBattista

It was Frieda Lawrence who wanted the sequel to *The Rainbow* entitled *Dies Irae*, the Days of Wrath, the Final Days. Lawrence preferred the less apocalyptically charged *Women in Love*. Frieda's suggestion preserved for Lawrence's proposed "double" novel the grace of symmetry: Genesis and Apocalypse, the total history of Creation recapitulated and reinterpreted in modern times. *The Rainbow* was a novel chronicling the creation of the first woman in "the Essential Days"; *Women in Love* actually concerns the destiny of the last men in the final days: the death of Gerald Crich, the Nietzschean captain of industry; and the eclipse, whether temporary or terminal, of Rupert Birkin, the artist as social prophet and sage.

As a novelist and polemicist of the final days, Lawrence always insists, as he does in *Fantasia of the Unconscious*, that he is merely "trying to stammer out the first terms of a forgotten knowledge." For him, the first terms are always the primary principles of a metaphysic that is both comprehended and lived: "Men live and see according to some gradually developing and gradually withering vision. This vision exists also as a dynamic idea or metaphysics—exists first as such. Then it is unfolded into life and art. Our vision, our belief, our metaphysic is wearing woefully thin, and the art is wearing absolutely threadbare. We have no future; neither for our hopes nor our aims nor our art." In Lawrence's view, the dependency of art on a metaphysic, its secondariness before the larger forms of an authentic cosmology, is compen-

From *D. H. Lawrence: A Centenary Consideration*, edited by Peter Balbert and Phillip L. Marcus. © 1985 by Cornell University Press.

sated by art's transparency as the expressive medium for an unknown time, what Lawrence calls the "next future," an odd and apparently redundant locution that testifies to the Lawrencian belief that the future is what succeeds the present yet remains unconditioned by it. The present always contains the possibility of a "renewed chaos" from which emerges "the strangeness and rainbow-change of ever-renewed creative civilisations." As a symbolic object, the rainbow recommends itself as a model of historical development because it possesses both the aura of natural phenomena—hence its familiar and reassuring presence in the world's landscapes—and the strangeness of a numinous object invested with the prestige and power of the sacred, a promissory sign of the eternal world keeping faith with the world of time.

However, the "earth's new architecture" announced in *The Rainbow*'s final transformative vision of "a world built up in a living fabric of Truth, fitting to the over-arching heaven" is only experienced through the visionary ecstasies of the redeemed female. The New Eve always precedes the newly awakened Adam into a paradise of fulfilled desire; the Old Adam, that typological and typical Lawrencian hero, dies belatedly, if at all. Men in *The Rainbow*, as in *Women in Love*, are the preservers of the past; they are the lovers of the Gothic "which always asserted the broken desire of mankind," abjuring the spectacle of "Absolute Beauty." Most of Lawrence's men are the artists of the elegiac for whom "a temple is never perfectly a temple, till it is ruined". For such men, the sublime is ineluctably connected with the sites of the ruined past.

The Rainbow thus adumbrates the sexual dialectic that informs the struggle for imaginative mastery in its successor fiction. But unlike Lawrence's generational novel, *Women in Love* places its human subjects against a backdrop largely absent from *The Rainbow*, the "great retrogression" of mankind into a "process of active corruption." Lawrence insists on distinguishing between the degenerate metaphysic that precipitates the historical decline of the West and his own resurgent sexual symbolism that issues from this renewed chaos born of decay. From the opening chapter of *The Rainbow* through the last major polemic of his career, *Apocalypse*, Lawrence argues, both as a predicate of his metaphysic and as a structure of his fiction that, "when there is a touch of true symbolism, it is not of the nature of a ruin or a remains embedded in the present structure, it is rather an archaic reminiscence." Finally, it is Lawrence's generic memory that determines the forgotten knowledge his novels seek to revive and communicate. And it is his controversial genius that traces all inherited symbolic codes to their origin in sexual difference.

II

The first terms of a forgotten knowledge are summarily recalled in the foreword to *Women in Love*, where Lawrence announces the absolute equality of desire and destiny as coefficients in the balanced equation of creation. The business of the novelist is to express this true fate: "The creative, spontaneous soul sends forth its promptings of desire and aspiration in us. These promptings are our true fate, which is our business to fulfil. A fate dictated from outside, from theory or from circumstance, is a false fate." In his "Study of Thomas Hardy," Lawrence had complained that the novels of the great metaphysical realists Hardy and Tolstoy projected a false rather than a true image of fate by confusing the individual's war against society with the individual's struggle with God. The novels of classical realism are predicated on a false judgment and a fatal imagining of necessity "where transgression against the social code is made to bring destruction, as though the social code worked our irrevocable fate." Exhaustive criticism of Hardy's characters, Lawrence maintained, "would fill the Judgment book," a final accounting of life novelistically rendered. Unable to liberate themselves from "the greater idea of self-preservation, which is formulated in the State, in the whole modelling of the community," Hardy's heroes and heroines are doomed to perish in the wilderness: "This is the tragedy of Hardy, always the same: the tragedy of those who, more or less pioneers, have died in the wilderness, whither they had escaped for free action, after having left the walled security, and the comparative imprisonment, of the established convention."

Hardy's walled city is the novelistic space defined by the false fate dictated by theory (religious or biological determinism), or by circumstance (society in its practical and moral forms). The wilderness is the precarious open that designates the creative prodigalities of the eternal origin whose spontaneous activities always impress us as "the waste enormity of Nature." But waste, Blakean excess, is the principle that rules in nature and authorizes what Lawrence insists is the "greater morality" of unfathomed Nature. In the true Judgment Book, *Women in Love*, unfathomed Nature becomes the backdrop of the lesser morality play enacted in that walled city, the novel of manners (with its central plot—the double love stories of Birkin and Ursula, Gerald and

Gudrun). It would take, as Lawrence well knew, a radical revisioning of novelistic convention to release his characters from the established representations of life. But to reform generic conventions is, of course, to subject novelistic characters to yet another set of conventions (however "natural" their unfolding) and therefore, potentially, to a false fate.

Lawrence ignores the paradox at the novel's beginning, but it reappears to exact its full metaphysical payment at the novel's ending. The opening chapter, "Sisters," echoes, with characteristic Lawrencian self-overcoming, *The Rainbow*'s familial and generational interest in a female destiny. Yet this apparent continuity disguises a real disjunction between the initial and final segments of the double novel. In *Women in Love*'s original opening, the canceled prologue, the state of the male soul, the sexual torments of Rupert Birkin, was symptomatic of modernist dis-ease. Birkin's obsession was with the male body, "whilst he studied the women as *sisters*, knowing their meaning and intents" (emphasis added): "It was the men's physique which held the passion and mystery to him. The women he seemed to be kin to, he looked for the soul in them." Birkin's erotic longings merely duplicate, under the sign of sexual difference, the very soul/body dualism that his sexual ideal would abolish: "to love completely, in one and the same act: both body and soul at once." Women will appear in *Women in Love* as sisters, but they are no longer represented as Birkin's spiritual kin. If writers shed sicknesses in books, as Lawrence claimed, it is Lawrence's own soulfulness that *Women in Love* exorcises. The novel consciously disavows the knowledge of the female soul acquired in the writing of *The Rainbow*. It restores to women their mystery and freedom as novelistic subjects whose meaning and intents cannot, as the prologue mistakenly implied, be foreknown.

The passional mystery of female desire is renewed in the opening discussion between Gudrun and Ursula about their marriage "prospects." To marry or not to marry—that is the question that conventionally defines the choices open to novelistic heroines. But never has the dilemma been formulated in such pained alternatives: Gudrun ironically insisting that marriage, whatever the desire or the fitness of the individuals, is "bound to be an experience of some sort," and Ursula, in her first display of apocalyptic thinking, suggesting that marriage is "more likely the end of experience."

The marriage question is not just linked to the modernist crisis of disassociation and anomie but precipitates it. Nietzsche asserts in that gnomic book, *Twilight of the Idols*, that "modern" marriage and its supporting mythology of Romantic love bear witness to the decadence in the modern's "valuating instinct," a spiritual decline so pronounced that the modern "*instinctively prefer[s]* that which leads to dissolution, that which hastens the end." The objection to modern marriage lies not in marriage but in modernity, which has lost the beneficial instincts out "of which institutions grow, out of which the *future* grows": "The rationale of marriage lay in its indissolubility in principle: it thereby acquired an accent which could *make itself heard* against the accidents of feeling, passion, and the moment." For Lawrence, who like Nietzsche desires a permanent marriage not susceptible to the vagaries of passion, feeling, or the moment, marriage is also the final test of the instinct for life, the modern riddle whose solution would unveil the mystery of being. Marriage, he claimed, is the great puzzle of modern times, its sphinx riddle. "Solve it or be torn to pieces" is the decree.

Failure to solve the riddle of marriage entails the ritual penalty known as *sparagmos*, the dismemberment of the sacred body, without the ritualistic consolations and controls of ancient Dionysian rites. Modern attitudes toward marriage inevitably fragment the unitary fullness of being into subjective particles, novelistic (Jamesian) "points of view" instead of comprehensive cosmologies. It is at this point that Ursula and Gudrun begin taking "last stands" before they need to do so, a symptom of their fall into the fragmented world of modernity. " 'When it comes to the point, one isn't even tempted—oh, if I were tempted, I'd marry like a shot.—I'm only tempted *not* to.' The faces of both sisters suddenly lit up with amusement. 'Isn't it an amazing thing,' cried Gudrun, 'how strong the temptation is, not to!' They both laughed, looking at each other. In their hearts they were frightened."

The exchange of secret looks, "whilst each sister vaguely considered her fate," communicates more than the malaise of diminished desire; it introduces into the novel's emergent sexual dialectic a primary female negativity before any external forces of prohibition or interdiction are called into play. This negativity, registered in the sisters' denial of their own possible future, is essentially temporal; it signals a collapse of the time needed for the self's unfolding into the compacted and airless space of irony (Gudrun) or anomie (Ursula). Both responses measure the distance separating female desire from the established familial system of filiation and alliance. This distance between desire and the concrete forms of marriage Lawrence's novel must either traverse or abolish entirely.

"Sisters" centers on the radical isolation of the modern woman, alienated from marriage and its central affirmations: the principle of existential security—the promise of indissolubility—and the principle of temporal security, the insured destiny of future generations. The next chapter in *Women in Love*, "Shortlands" (the manor of the Crich dynasty), considers the same problem, but from the perspective of the male will. Lawrence dramatizes in the career of Gerald Crich the peculiarly modern tragedy of the anarchic Dionysian spirit trying to express itself in the Apollonian (degraded) forms of industrial production. Gerald reminds Ursula "of Dionysus, because his hair was really yellow, his figure so full and laughing"; this reminder anticipates the male fate he must reenact: the modern god dying in the Nordic rite of ice annihilation. At issue in Gerald's destiny is the very meaning of "purpose" in the modern world, an issue addressed in the Lawrencian critique of work, the activity by which man, directed by the spontaneous aspirations of his creative soul, both reclaims his past and organizes his future.

Man works, writes Lawrence in his "Study of Thomas Hardy," because the source of his life is overfull and thus "presses for utterance." Weltschmerz and other "unlocalized pains" signify the pressures within man to "produce" himself. Work therefore constitutes both an inherent passion, a craving "to produce, to create, to be as God," and a faulty mimesis, for in craving to be as God, man can only repeat and reproduce "the movement life made in its initial passage, the movement life still makes, and will continue to make, as a habit, the movement already made so unthinkably often that rather than a movement it has become a state, a condition of all life; it has become matter, or the force of gravity, or cohesion, or heat, or light. These old, old habits of life man rejoices to rediscover in all their detail."

Work entails a conscious reminiscence of those generative movements that have congealed into immemorial "habits" that constitute the given, known conditions of nature: matter, gravity, cohesion, heat, light. The purpose of work is thus present in its basic form as *repetition*, "the repetition of some one of those rediscovered movements, the enacting of some part imitated from life, the attaining of a similar result as life attained." The motive of labor should be consonant with the meaning of work: "to bring all life into the human consciousness."

The mystic harmony between knowledge and life that obtains in the truly creative work is never realized in *Women in Love*. Lawrence's philosophy of work, derived from his reading of Hardy, finds expression only in its demonic opposite: the mechanical philosophy justifying the "life-work" of Gerald Crich. Lawrence, in a rare moment of conventional psychologizing, exposes the grounds of Gerald's savage materialism, tracing it to an early repression of his authentic desire for the epic existence of Homeric days: "During his childhood and his boyhood he had wanted a sort of savagedom. The days of Homer were his ideal, when a man was chief of an army of heroes, or spent his years in wonderful Odyssey." Gerald's drive to impose his will on the material universe is analyzed as a corrupt form of quixotic idealism. His idealizing compulsion, unlike Quixote's inventive madness, seeks to subjugate the world with "the sword of mechanical necessity" rather than with the broadsword of romance. But like all mad constructionists, Gerald elaborates a system of life that is internally consistent but weakly founded, predicated as it is on two faulty acts of translation—Gerald's mistaking the mystic word "harmony" for the practical word "organization" and his grotesque mistranslation of the godhead into pure mechanism: "He found his eternal and his infinite in the pure machine-principle of perfect coordination into one pure, complex infinitely repeated motion, like the spinning of a wheel: but a productive spinning, as the revolving of the universe may be called a productive spinning, a productive repetition through eternity, to infinity. And this is the God-motion, this productive repetition ad infinitum. And Gerald was the God for the machine, Deus ex Machina."

Not just the echo of Blake's Satanic Mills but the entire antirationalist tradition empowers Lawrence's parody of the materialist analytics that makes the godhead immanent in the world's material motions. Lawrence appropriates Blake's critique in his own polemical diagnosis of the "pure orders" valorized by rationalist metaphysics, the ideology whose historical products—the Krupp Mills, German militarism, and "the sick Man of Europe"—are fabled in the family chronicle of the Crich dynasty, from its sick and dying patriarch, Thomas Crich, to its Bismarckian savior, Gerald Crich. In fact, this historical dimension of the novel is so obvious that, like the Great War, its informing presence can, as Lawrence said, merely be taken for granted.

III

I began my treatment of *Women in Love* with mention of its initial chapters, "Sisters" and "Shortlands," because these early installments recapitulate the old novelistic themes that the unfolding narrative will seek to work through until they are either transmuted into something "new" or are dispersed by the energy of Lawrence's own apocalyptic imaginings. I have perhaps reductively identified these old themes as marriage and work, the private and public destinies apportioned to novelistic character. The novel's visionary plot to inaugurate a genuinely free, unpredictable course of narrative development actually commences with the third chapter, "Class-Room." "Class-Room" initiates the novel's real effort at a new beginning, a radical departure from the moribund traditions of realist fiction.

The formal attempt to purge the novel of its sentimental and sickly conventions is thematized in the personal drama enacted in "Class-Room": Birkin's attempt to dissassociate himself from Hermione, both as a lover and as a demonic double who mimics his ideas on spontaneous animal joy. Hermione is a Cassandra, but unlike the ancient prophetess whose knowledge is authentic and whose words are discredited, the modern Cassandra is a spectral presence whose agonies result not from the ironic reception of her predictions but from the ironic distance between her speech and the knowledge she would communicate. Her ecstatic language is derided as the "worst and last form of intellectualism," her transports as the convulsions of a will that can only experience the "animalistic" nature of the body as a mental abstraction. Hermione is not only a Cassandra but the Lady of Shalott, another cursed female visionary whose will-bound imagination condemns her to a mirror world of shadows, that will never materialize: "You've got that mirror, your own fixed will, your immortal understanding, your own tight conscious world, and there is nothing beyond it."

Birkin's struggle with Hermione, whose rhetoric shadows Birkin's in the vampirish form of unconscious parody and conscious mockery, and who reflects his fear of self-mirroring, is thus part of the larger struggle the novel seeks to portray: the "struggle for verbal consciousness," as Lawrence identifies it in his foreword. Only the verbalizing "instinct" possesses the eruptive force needed to reclaim the past and to project a future in one totalizing movement. The ceaseless promptings of desire *must* find their way into language where they can be materialized into living forms, or else they will languish in the mind. Lawrence's famous manifesto on novelistic character insists on replacing "the old forms and sentimentalities" of novelistic discourse with this new *materializing* language:

You mustn't look in my novel for the old stable ego of the character. There is another ego according to whose action the individual is unrecognizable, and passes through, as it were, allotropic states which it needs a deeper sense than any we've been used to exercise, to discover are states of the same single radically-unchanged element. (Like as diamond and coal are the same pure single element of carbon. The ordinary novel would trace the history of the diamond—but I say "diamond, what! This is carbon." And my diamond might be coal or soot, and my theme is carbon.)

To chronicle this allotropic development, in which the elemental ego passes through the successive stages of its potentiality, Lawrence appropriates an archaic language that posited the existence of multiple states, the language of totemism. Totemism is the atavistic language by which the constituent elements that collectively compose the given themes of any culture find their living expression. Totemism provides a serviceable nomenclature for an otherwise "unrecognizable" and therefore potentially *unrepresentable* Lawrencian ego because, as Birkin implies in the chapter entitled "Totem," totemic objects convey the complete truth of a "state" without vitiating or compromising it under the morally static signs of analytic language.

Lawrence, of course, read widely in the burgeoning anthropological literature (Frazer, Weston, Tylor, Harrison) that helped inspire the pancultural myths of modernist works such as *Ulysses* and *The Waste Land* or *Totem and Taboo* (1913). His particular interest in totemism may have derived from totemism's privileged position in the anthropological descriptions of primitive cultures. According to Frazer's *Totemism and Exogamy*, religion itself emerged out of the disruption and decay of totemism; and totemism survives as an elemental remainder and reminder of older social forms in the "later phase of religious evolution." Totemism's capacity to survive as an "archaic reminiscence" of the collective mind thus accounts for its pancultural *and* panhistorical vitality. As Frazer observes, "There is nothing in the institution itself incompatible with the pastoral, agricultural, even the commercial and industrial modes of life, since in point of fact it remains to this day in vogue among hunters, fishers, farmers, traders, weavers, leather-makers, and stone-masons, not to mention the less reputable professions of quackery, fortune-telling, and robbery."

The real appeal of totemism for Lawrence, whatever its diversionary interest as a patron institution for quacks and fortune tellers, is that it constitutes a system of relationships—animalistic, spiritual, and social—that honors the law of difference, primarily through the stabilizing institution of exogamy. Lawrence's criticism of the modern democratic "isms" (Fabianism, liberalism, socialism, and communism) is that each system advocates a social state based on the utopian goal of material and spiritual equality. Speaking through the bitter declamations of Birkin, Lawrence maintains that social life must reflect and foster the original and originating purpose of life: differentiation. "We are all abstractly or mathematically equal, if you like. Every man has hunger and thirst, two eyes, one nose and two legs. We're all the same in point of number. But spiritually, there is pure difference and neither equality nor inequality counts. It is upon these two bits of knowledge that you must found a state. . . . One man isn't any better than another, not because they are equal, but because they are intrinsically *other*, that there is no term of comparison." Equality is a theoretical construct abstracted out of the data of material necessity; hence Birkin banishes it to the realm of number, wherein its truth and utility, if any, are to be found. In the essay "Democracy," Lawrence converts the primal fact of Otherness into the first term of his "metaphysics of presence." "Our life, our being depends upon the incalculable issue from the central Mystery into indefinable *presence*. This sounds in itself an abstraction. But not so. It is rather the perfect absence of abstraction. The central Mystery is no generalized abstraction. It is each man's primal original soul or self, within him.

The metaphysics of presence demands a language purified of any false "term of comparison" if it is to preserve the inviolability of its "central Mystery." Yet how is the absolute law of otherness to be fulfilled (or even monitored) in the verbal and social contracts of individuals and to retain its ontological status as "the undefinable"? This problem Birkin himself encounters in a rather playful dialectical conversation with Ursula about the "nature" of daisies.

> "They are nice flowers," he said, her emotional tones putting a constraint on him.
> "You know that a daisy is a company of florets, a concourse, become individual. Don't the botanists put it highest in the line of development? I believe they do."
> "The compositae, yes, I think so," said Ursula, who was

never very sure of anything. Things she knew perfectly well, at one moment, seemed to become doubtful the next.

"Explain it so, then," he said. "The daisy is a perfect little democracy, so it's the highest of flowers, hence its charm."

"No," she cried, "no—never. It isn't democratic."

"No," he admitted. "It's the golden mob of the proletariat, surrounded by a showy white fence of the idle rich."

"How hateful—your hateful social orders!" she cried.

"Quite! It's a daisy—we'll leave it alone."

The ease with which Birkin can postulate the terms of comparison between democracy and the composite structure of the daisy, the facility with which he can transform the daisy into an emblem of the class divisions segregating the proletariat from the idle rich testify to the seductiveness of analogical language. Resisting the temptations of false resemblance is part of the struggle for verbal consciousness that the novel recounts. Birkin must forebear seeking explanations in the concave mirror of false analogy; therein lies the significance of his deferential act in the presence of the daisy: "It's a daisy—we'll leave it alone." The verbal gesture is slight, even comic, but Birkin honors the uniqueness of the daisy as the absolute *other*.

Lawrence's rhetoric of difference found inspiration in the naturalistic language of totemism. Totemism establishes a classificatory system of relationships predicated on the imaginary brotherhood of resemblances in difference. Totemic language externalizes the "primal, original soul within"; it signifies the living realities issuing from the depths of the central mystery and posits their organic relationships. The authority of this totemic identity justifies Lawrence's banishment of the old "stable ego" hypostasized in the novelistic cult of "personality" and the "great Mind" from which it descends.

> You can't have life two ways. Either everything is created from the mind, downwards; or else everything preceeds [sic] from the creative quick, outwards into exfoliation and blossom. Either a great Mind floats in space: God, the Anima Mundi, the Oversoul, drawing with a pair of compasses and making everything to scale, even emotions and self-conscious effusions; or else creation proceeds from the forever inscrutable quicks of living beings, men, women, animals, plants. The actual living quick itself is alone the creative reality.

The struggle for verbal consciousness is waged in the unspoken battle raging between Birkin, the metaphysician of presence, who celebrates the inscrutable quick of living beings, and Gudrun, that formidable apostle of Mind for whom the world is a spectacle of descending creations, life defined (and degenerating) downward, abstracted, "preconcluded." Committed to the notion of personality, she regards the human being "as a complete figure, like a character in a book, or a subject in a picture, or a marionette in a theatre, a finished creation." When she sees Gerald for the first time, the novel, adopting her mode of perception, lapses into the language typical of "old" narrative habits of representation. Gerald is described in terms of externals, "a fair, sun-tanned type, rather above middle height, well-made, and almost exaggeratedly well-dressed": "But about him also was the strange, guarded look, the unconscious glisten, as if he did not belong to the same creation as the people about him."

Gudrun can only express the unconscious glisten that identifies Gerald as *another*, not the *same* creation as the fixed and finished characters about him, by invoking his totemic reality: " 'His totem is the wolf,' she repeated to herself. 'His mother is an old, unbroken wolf.' And then she experienced a keen paroxysm, a transport, as if she had made some incredible discovery, known to nobody else on earth." Gudrun's "powerful apprehension" of Gerald's essence is not the result of conscious metaphor making, that is, metaphor making as an exercise of the will intent on connecting the known with the unknown. "His totem is the wolf" is rather a kind of double metaphor, the first part, totem, assimilating even as it traverses the second part, wolf. Totemistically, Gerald is that doubly unknown and undefinable reality, wolf manifest. Wolf is the ancestral and universal reality struggling to express itself through him. The totemic depths of Gerald's individuality are brought to the narrative surface through a process of charged language that does not bother to discriminate between generative forces and their individual manifestations. Lawrence's language here is designed to radicalize metaphor and all other "terms of comparison" by eliminating the mediating middle term in the vital transfer of meaning from the depths to the surfaces. He wants his language to destroy or incapacitate that part of the verbal consciousness, best represented in the "mind" of Gudrun, which habitually employs language to encircle, complete, and define (fix) the real.

Thus language determines novelistic destiny in *Women in Love*. The novel's climactic moment of reckoning may be seen in the great chapter "Gudrun in the Pompadour," which stages the secular specta-cle of the Logos "harrowing hell," Birkin's excoriation of the decadent Halliday crowd with his prophetic "letter" proclaiming the unalterable law that will prevail in *Dies Irae*: "the Flux of corruption . . . , the reducing back of the created body of life." The episode's dramatic power issues from the charged interplay between the novel's two competing "artists," the absent Birkin (present by virtue of his jere-miad on modernism) and Gudrun, the fashioner of miniatures, the respecter of the old virtues and corrupt privileges of the dead letter "I," and Birkin's only real rival in *Women in Love*.

Gudrun incarnates "a desire for the reduction process in oneself" that Birkin identifies as the sign of modern decadence. Her art repre-sents "the process of active corruption" that results in Baudelairian "fleurs du mal," those (literary) flowers of evil that hauntingly contrast with Birkin's pristine daisies. When Gudrun overhears the Halliday party ridiculing Birkin's "genuine letter," she goes over to their table, retrieves the letter, and walks out of the Pompadour "in her measured fashion." In the ethos of a traditional novel, Gudrun's act is praisewor-thy, a dignified defense of a friend's right to privacy, the decorous rescue of a private letter from mocking public scrutiny. But Gudrun is defending values that Lawrence cannot and will not endorse: the value of privacy and family loyalty, the affiliative ties that defined the obliga-tions and prescribed the roles of an "older," stable ego. Her act is justly recorded in the language of the narrative commentary as a misdeed. Gudrun rescues the letter at the expense of its spirit, and the novel, after her dramatic act of retrieval and repossession, reverts to the literalism of "realistic" description in narrating her triumphant exit:

> From Halliday's table came half articulate cries, then some-body booed, then all the fal end of the place began booing after Gudrun's retreating form. She was fashionably dressed in blackish-green and silver, her hat was brilliant green, like the sheen on an insect, but the brim was soft dark green, a falling edge with fine silver, her coat was dark green, bril-liantly glossy, with a high collar of grey fur, and great fur cuffs, the edge of her dress showed silver and black velvet, her stockings and shoes were silver grey. She moved with slow, fashionable indifference to the door.

Gudrun's movements are tracked in this pure description of sur-faces, a narrative gesture on Lawrence's part that is at best supererogatory and at worst damning. Gudrun moves within the colorful modalities of self-display, while the real existential issue of Birkin is nakedness. Birkin argues with Gerald and Ursula about the dispensability of clothes; he wrestles naked with Gerald in "Gladiatorial"; and he and Ursula ritually disrobe in "Excurse" to experience the "unrevealed nudity" of the mystic body of reality. Gudrun in the Pompadour acts out the old ethics—and psychology—of self-presentation; Birkin yearns for a kind of psychic nakedness in the reality of human encounters. Gudrun defines and defends the rhetoric of finality, the aesthetic of the finished and polished creation. Birkin attempts to stammer out the words of a new rhetoric of futurity in the last facts of nakedness. The novel as it nears its conclusion represents a battle between these two rhetorics, a struggle between Gudrun and Birkin, not just for mastery over the novelistic spaces they occupy, but over the soul of the last modern hero—Gerald Crich. Their competition generates a system of warring metaphysics (neither fully articulated nor fully sufficient), and the aesthetics appropriate to each: Birkin, the voyager into the unknown, the Hardyean "pioneer" who journeys into the fruitful wastes seeking his destiny in what he calls "mystic marriage"; Gudrun, the "Glucksritter," riding the unstable currents of fashion, the Eternal Feminine pursuing her own degradation as the whore of Fortune, whose vehicle is the wheel of mechanical transformation.

IV

Birkin's salvationist reimagining of the creative life is nowhere as dramatically figured as in "Moony," Lawrence's most controlled and condensed narrative meditation on modern love purged of its Meredithian "sickly cant." "Moony" describes Birkin's obsessive disfigurement of the image of the moon reflected in the surfaces of a pond. This lunar reflection is not for him a natural icon for the order of mutability but a demonized image of Cybele, the "accursed Syria Dea" of Asiatic mother cults. In an effort to discharge the powers of darkness gathering force within him, Birkin throws stone after stone into the motionless pond, turning it into "a battlefield of broken lights and shadows," a field of "white fragments" that mirrors his own obsession with those disintegrative processes that may portend, for all their negativity, a positive struggle to emerge from the womb of creation. Yet the moon's image remains unviolated—Nature sees to it that the "scattered fragments" course their way back to the still center: "He saw the

moon regathering itself insidiously, saw the heart of the rose intertwining vigorously and blindly, calling back the scattered fragments,
winning home the fragments, in a pulse and in effort of return."
Sparagmos to *nostos:* the winning home of fragments—that, of course,
is the desired homecoming at the thematic and mythic heart of modern
narratives from Joyce's *Ulysses* to Beckett's grimly ironic, vagrant
fictions of disintegration. Winning home is the telos of modern art—to
repair, no matter how tempting the urge to fall "back in panic," the
"ragged rose," Dante's rose of the World. Winning home is what
Birkin sees as "the remaining way" open to those weary of contem-
plating the modern mysteries of dissolution: "There was another way,
the way of freedom. There was the paradisal entry into pure, single
being, the individual soul taking precedence over love and desire for
union, stronger than any pangs of emotion, a lovely state of free
proud-singleness, which accepted the obligation of the permanent connection with others, and with the others, submits to the yoke and leash
of love, but never forfeits its own proud individual singleness, even
while it loves and yields." Birkin, however, remains unsure whether
his vision of free proud singleness is "only an idea, or . . . the interpretation of a profound yearning." Love must be experienced as a "travelling together," a mobile nostos, an exploratory way, never a final
destination. Lawrence's novel never abandons its desire to see the
elemental ego find its own way into the unknown, its true fate.

The "love" story of Birkin and Ursula embedded in and illumi-
nating the dark heart of *Women in Love* represents Lawrence's attempt
to render the great, perhaps the last, epic adventure of modernity—the
exploration of the as yet unknown. This love story generically attains
its consummatory moment of winning home, its paradisal entry into a
new world, in the chapter peripatetically entitled "Excurse," in which
Birkin proposes to Ursula the terms of his star marriage, terms she
will come to accept as the liberating fatality of love. The chapter opens
with Birkin's decision to renounce the tutelage of Luck as a vulgar
minister of destiny; he refuses to accept that life is "a series of accidents—
like a picaresque novel." "Excurse" thus becomes one of Lawrence's
most successful fictional representations of a "generic" self-overcoming.
The picaresque, the narrative of human destiny imaged forth as a series
of accidents originating in the contingencies of history, social caste,
and economic conditions, is invoked only to be revoked as a fictional
legacy that validates a "false fate." In "Excurse" the promise of *The
Rainbow* is realized: Ursula's "new knowledge of eternity in the flux of

time" is fulfilled in her *internally* apprehended knowledge of "the inevitability and beauty of fate, fate which one asks for, which one accepts in full" and in "this star-equilibrium which alone is freedom."

Yet despite her revelatory vision of a self-generated fate, the true "fate which one asks for," not the untoward destiny one struggles against, like a picaresque heroine, Ursula does not always accede to the conditions of her newfound freedom in star-equilibrium. The reason is partly that Lawrence prefers to leave his characters in uncertainty and partly that Ursula remains for Lawrence totemically bound to her essence as Magna Mater, the Great Mother who insists on pressing for a reactionary and limited kind of love, love as ecstatic fusion. Like all of Lawrence's early heroines, from Mrs. Morel to Anna "Victrix" Brangwen, Ursula has a predilection for a consuming romance whose central episode is the idyll of a sexual paradise regained. Generically, romance is the narrative form that seeks to cancel out the differences separating love and its objects. For Lawrence, it is *the* female form of imaginative desire, born out of the female will to absorb the "Other" in the all-comprehending womb. The Great Mother would reclaim all individualized life into the undifferentiated Source, drawing all articulated meanings and distinctions into herself. For Ursula, who might be won over by love's (and Birkin's) excursionary nature, intercourse is still initially and perhaps finally the act of homecoming, the winning home of the errant male.

Birkin's suspicions that the Magna Mater's lust for "unspeakable intimacies" lurks behind every female's urge to "mate" leave him dissatisfied with mystic marriage as the controlling metaphor for his transvaluing vision of life. Because marriage is disposed, by the sheer force of institutional inertia and by the reactionary demands of the "feminine" will to enforce a unity where none should exist, Birkin advocates the complementary, revolutionary relation of *Blutbrüderschaft*. The truly subversive content of *Women in Love*, its well-conceived threat to the conventional attitudes toward human relationships propagated by the "bourgeois" novel, is in expanding the idea of spiritual mating to encompass a male-to-male relation, a broader and less interested relation than the "égoïsme à deux" or "hunting in couples" that characterizes modern marriages.

Birkin's rite of "bloodbrotherhood" is authorized both by his personal desire for a male relationship and by the more utilitarian need to populate the "new world" of his visions with as yet undefined human constellations in supposed star-equilibrium. But beneath Birkin's ideological justification for such a male rite as a "new utterance" issuing out of life's creative mysteries, there abides the epic striving condensed and displaced in the obsessions of Birkin's *Salvator Mundi* complex: his classical yearning for the "Gladiatorial" *virtus* embodied in the Homeric figure of Gerald Crich. Of course Gerald has ostensibly betrayed his heroic nature by dedicating himself to the "established world" and its decadent, moribund orders "in which he did not livingly believe." Conventional marriage would prove "the seal of his condemnation": it would condemn him to the underworld "like a soul damned but living forever in damnation." Birkin's offer of *Blutbrüderschaft* is the redemptive alliance that Gerald considers in the chapter "Marriage or Not": "If he pledged himself with the man he would later be able to pledge himself with the woman: not merely in legal marriage, but in absolute, mystic marriage." But Gerald declines Rupert's offer, whether because of "unborn, absent volition or of atrophy" Birkin declines to speculate and Lawrence refuses to say.

Of course Birkin's revolutionary offer to rescue Gerald from his impending doom is exposed as an illusory choice in the novel's depiction of the Final Days. For Gerald has already made his choice in the previous chapter, prophetically entitled "Death and Love." The death of his father brings Gerald to a crisis state in which, poised on the edge of the grave, the image of the perilous void, he "must take direction." Crisis, as Frank Kermode reminds us, citing the pun of St. John, comprises a moment both of judgment and of separation. For Gerald the moment of crisis resolves itself in a decision to separate himself from the "one center" authorized and inhabited by his father—"the unseen, raw grave": "No, he had nothing to stay here for." He then forms his "dangerous resolve"—to go to Gudrun, "persistently, like a wind, straight forwards, as if to his fate." But this resolution issues in a false "separation" of love and death. Even as Gerald enters Gudrun's bedroom seeking comfort in love's restorative rites, he tracks in the cold clay of the grave. Death and love become dialectically wedded, composing the signs that dictate Gerald's true fate. Whatever Birkin might do to oppose it, Gerald is set on an irreversible course of self-destruction. In a letter to John Middleton Murry, Lawrence describes the limits of his own revolutionary vision of the millennium when the world will be repopulated with the new men and women of his imaginings: "I think that one day—before so very long—we shall come together again, this time on a living earth, not in the world of destructive going apart. I believe we shall do things together, and be happy. But we can't dictate the terms, nor the times. It has to come to pass in us. Yet one has the hope, that is the reality."

The *Götterdämmerung* finale of the novel confirms Lawrence's intuition that neither the terms nor the times ordained for the world's "destructive going apart" can be dictated by the human will—either the regenerate will of the prophet, or the corrupt will of the insane "ecstatics," like Gudrun and Loerke, who herald the dawn of "the obscene beyond." Birkin's vision thus acquires an ambiguous status in the novel's already tortuous eschatology—it expresses the hope for, not the imminence of, a new creative order. This hope diminishes as the novel relentlessly moves toward its last days, whose end terms are dominated not by Birkin's visionary excursions but by the sick "love story" of Gudrun and Gerald.

The destinies of Gerald and Gudrun constitute, as Lawrence once wrote of Dostoevsky's novels, "great parables . . . but false art." Their love story represents, that is, the dead life and the moribund forms of older (tragic) narratives whose formal integrity conformed to a deterministic notion of historical causality. This formalism appears in an early exchange between Gudrun and Gerald: "You have struck the first blow," Gerald reminds Gudrun, to which she responds with "confident assurance," "And I shall strike the last." That Gudrun's threat sounds like a prediction is a sign of her (and the reader's) confidence in the symmetry intrinsic to the resolutions of the classical novel. Lawrence's own analysis of Dostoevsky's "parables" helps illuminate his unwilling incorporation of this "false" yet inevitable formalism into the last stages of *Women in Love*. Writing again to Murry, who was working on a study of Dostoevsky, Lawrence observes: "The Christian ecstasy leads to imbecility (the Idiot). The sensual ecstasy leads to universal murder: for mind, the acme of sensual ecstasy lies in *devouring* the other, even in the pleasures of love, it is a devouring, like a tiger drinking blood (Rogozhin). But the full sensual ecstasy is never reached except by Rogozhin in murdering Nastasya. It is nipped in the last stages by the *will*, the social will."

This Dostoevskian insight shadows Lawrence's representation of Thomas Crich's sentimental Christianity and Gudrun's demonic sensuality. Christian ecstasy, which Thomas Crich seeks through his self-abnegating charities and his sentimental, "democratic" politics, leads to his final imbecility and the slow stupor of lingering death. Sensual ecstasy is the special lust of Gudrun, whose face betrays the insane will of the "demoniacal ecstatic" and whose love affair with Gerald, like her nostalgic fascination with the underworld of his mines, grows out of her desire to experience the "perfect voluptuous finality." Her affair with Gerald must end with her triumph in "the last stages" and, as the Dostoevskian parable instructs, in sensually gratifying murder.

Lawrence's unwilling but not inadvertent accommodation of Dostoevsky's spiritual determinism *as the only possible* resolution to his visionary narrative is also reflected in the larger structural configurations of the novel. *Women in Love* begins with an unstable triangle—Hermione, Ursula, and Birkin—that Birkin attempts to replace with the transforming relationships comprehended in mystic marriage. But as the novel moves toward the Continent and into its *Götterdämmerung* phase, the generic imperative to observe certain novelistic symmetries begins to reassert itself. The novel's initial sexual triangle reappears in the parodic and demonic trinity of Loerke, Gudrun, and Gerald. Moreover, the novel also regresses to a formalist rigidity in echoing Birkin's vision of male love in Loerke's relation to Leitner, an alliance that demystifies Birkin's mystic sense of *Blutbrüderschaft* in the perversions of "ecstatic" and exploitive homosexuality.

To discredit the determinism that is overwhelming his narrative, Lawrence has Gudrun mock the conventional explanation that the violence called forth in the final stages of her battle with Gerald is due to the tensions and jealousies traditionally associated with the "eternal" love triangle: " 'A pretty little sample of the eternal triangle!' And she turned ironically away, because she knew that the fight had been between Gerald and herself and that the presence of the third party was a mere contingency—an inevitable contingency perhaps, but a contingency none the less. But let them have it as an example of the eternal triangle, the trinity of hate. It would be simpler for them." Gudrun's scathing dismissal of the idea that her triangular entanglements with Gerald and Loerke compose a trinity of hate, a demonic variation of the eternal triangle, is based on a quibble about the meaning and importance of "contingencies." But what does she, or even Lawrence, mean by the self-contradictory assertion that Loerke's presence operates as an "inevitable" contingency? How can a contingency be both accidental and forseeable, dependent on chance yet necessary as both a primary and secondary cause? What is important to Gudrun's self-interpretation is not her claim that her battle with Gerald represents a singular death struggle between two insane wills; rather, what emerges as significant and triumphant is Gudrun's power of dismissive irony, her tonal mastery over the reality of the last facts, the violent ends of *Dies Irae*.

In *Women in Love*, Gudrun's vision, the ironical vision of love and death, overwhelms the imaginations of the artist of life, Rupert Birkin. Birkin tries to inaugurate a reign of freedom, the new time of the transcendent individual who lives in close contact with the inexhaustible life source. Gudrun, with Loerke, her demonic consort, inaugurates the totalitarian regime of terror, the nightmare of history and historicism, the coming era of real social hatred. Gudrun's is a peculiarly "modern" madness, not the classical and even pathos-ridden madness of Hermione, who is partially redeemed by her mythic affinity with Cassandra. In her prophetic but unredeeming imagination, Gudrun confronts and then *becomes* the specter that haunts the modern mind, the specter of mechanical causation.

> Perhaps she was healthy. Perhaps it was only her unabatable health that left her so exposed to the truth. If she were sickly she would have her illusions, imaginations. As it was, there was no escape. She must always see and know and never escape. She could never escape. There she was, placed before the clock-face of life. . . . She was watching the fingers twitch across the eternal, mechanical, monotonous clock-face of time. She never really lived, she only watched. Indeed, she was like a little, twelve-hour clock, vis-à-vis with the enormous clock of eternity—there she was, like Dignity and Impudence, or Impudence and Dignity.

Gudrun identifies with the eternal repetition of the clock face as the internal principle of her existence, thus alienating herself from the nurturing and restorative cycles of natural time: hence "her unripening nights, her unfruitful slumbers." She is the mad prophetess who presides over the apocalyptic Terrors that proclaim the end of the world as a ceaseless duration. *Dies Irae* for Gudrun take the form of a perpetual *chronos*, to paraphrase Kermode's formulation of the modernist's "intemporal agony," chronos without kairos, without a transforming, all-reversing and all-renewing eruption of creative mystery into the remorseless chronicity of linear, clock-face time. Gudrun can neither envision nor hope for deliverance. She can only persist in fashioning the totalitarian, apocalyptic fantasies she plays out with Loerke, the "final craftsman" of "the last series of subtleties," who "did not deceive himself in the last issue":

> As for the future, that they never mentioned except one laughed out some mocking dream of the destruction of the

world by a ridiculous catastrophe of man's invention: a man
invented such a perfect explosive that it blew the earth in
two, and the two halves set off in different directions through
space, to the dismay of the inhabitants: or else the people of
the world divided into two halves, and each half decided *it*
was the perfect and right, the other half was wrong and
must be destroyed; so another end of the world.

Gudrun and Loerke translate the central rite of modernity—
sparagmos—into global and genocidal terms: the earth torn in two,
mankind's destructive dream of exterminating the ideologically corrupt other. As the final form in their last series of subtleties, Loerke
and Gudrun construct this mad parody that inverts Plato's myth of the
origin of sexual love in Zeus's punitive division of the original her-
maphroditic body into halves, who thereafter seek to reunite through
love. Time becomes a clock face onto which they project their false
"Dignity" and their true "Impudence" as artists of the obscene whose
ecstatic vision of the End finds its consummation in universal murder.

Gudrun's myth of finality is registered in the cold, life-betraying
voice of irony: "Everything turned to irony with her: the last flavour
of everything was ironical." Kierkegaard claimed that irony was "in
the strictest sense a mastered moment" and saw in the birth of ironic
consciousness "the absolute beginning of the personal life." For
Kierkegaard, irony is the baptism of human beginning; for Lawrence
irony is the last rites of the living-dead. That the creative moment
could in any way be limited to and defined by the needs and desires,
the dignities—and impudence—of the personal life is repugnant to his
metaphysical and rhetorical doctrines of impersonality. For Lawrence
language should adhere and inhere in the reality it denominates, in the
new utterances it struggles to deliver over to verbal consciousness
Irony, the conscious displacement of meaning from its vehicles of
expression, irony as the deliberate estrangement of essence and phenomena, is the last betrayal of the creative Source.

Gerald's death vindicates Gudrun's status as the ironical artist who
has mastered the creative moments immanent in the "time" of Nature.
It is Gudrun who regards Gerald's death as an inevitable contingency
attending the Final Days, a necessary but "barren tragedy" without
meaning or significance, but hers is the view of cold irony. It is at this
point that Birkin returns to the novel that he has abandoned (and that
has abandoned him) to contest Gudrun's ironical reading of Gerald's

death. He mourns the fallen hero and retreats, not behind the frigid dignities of irony, but into the enclosed and emotionally charged spaces of elegy: "I didn't want it to be like this." Ursula, to her horror, hears the accent of nostalgia in Birkin's valedictory lament and cannot help thinking of the Kaiser's "Ich habe es nicht gewollt." In exposing the historical retreat implicit in Birkin's elegiac meditations, Ursula argues for the "realities" honored in the resolutions of the classical novel and in so doing interprets Birkin's grief as a perversion, a refusal to accept the fate decreed by those impersonal forces that constitute the Real.

> "You can't have two kinds of love. Why should you!"
> "It seems as if I can't," he said. "Yet I wanted it."
> "You can't have it, because it's wrong, impossible," she said.
> "I don't believe that," he answered.

Women in Love thus represents and advances the modernist crisis of separation and judgment. Its *Götterdämmerung* finale envisions the last symmetries in the form of an impasse and an argument. Birkin's perverse insistence that his desire to "save" Gerald was not a false, nor even a barren, hope, but a living expression of his heart's desire, his true fate, is contrasted with Gudrun's grim, ironical view of necessity. His quarrel with Gudrun over the meaning of history is perhaps less threatening to his metaphysic than his argument with Ursula over the visionary possibility of *Blutbrüderschaft*, men wedded in purpose and in love. Both the historical impasse and the emotional argument remain unresolved, their outcome temporarily suspended by a narrative moratorium dictated by Birkin's grief and Lawrence's own need to reimagine the presence of the creative mystery that will "carry on the embodiment of creation" even if mankind is exterminated—or annihilates itself. The novel opens itself up to the future only by insisting on a kind of blank space in time, empty yet still capable of being filled with new utterances, "miraculous unborn species."

In an essay on modern painting, Lawrence pictured Cézanne's struggle with the visual clichés that composed the tainted inheritance, the corrupted legacy of pictorial form. His analysis illuminates and corresponds to Lawrence's own transvaluing critique of novelistic conventions. "In other pictures he seems to be saying: Landscape is not like this and not like this and not like this and not . . . etc.—and every *not* is a little blank space in the canvas, defined by the remains of an assertion. Sometimes Cézanne builds up a landscape essentially out of omissions. He puts fringes on the complicated vacuum of the cliché, so to speak, and offers us that. It is interesting in a repudiative fashion but it is not the new thing." *Women in Love*, despite its efforts to imagine and realize a "new thing," comes to rest on the fringe of the complicated vacuum of novelistic cliché. Birkin's belief that life need "not," is "not," like this and this—contains the remains of an assertion, but it is hard to determine whether his refusal to submit to Ursula's pragmatic and historical view of the limits of human desire is anything more than mental repudiation. *Women in Love* begins but cannot conclude Lawrence's own struggle with the memory of classical narrative, which trusted, not naively, but livingly, in a final day of historical reckoning. *Women in Love* is the Judgment Book that publishes the decrees of a Providence that Lawrence could neither ignore nor accept.

Chronology

<table>
<tr><td>1885</td><td>David Herbert Lawrence is born on September 11 in Eastwood, a Nottingham mining village, the fourth child of Arthur Lawrence, a coal miner, and Lydia Beardsall Lawrence, a former schoolteacher of lower-middle-class background.</td></tr>
<tr><td>1898–1901</td><td>Attends Nottingham High School on a County Council Scholarship.</td></tr>
<tr><td>1901</td><td>Meets Jessie Chambers, who becomes his childhood amour and the model for "Miriam Leivers" of Sons and Lovers; goes to work for a dealer in artificial limbs.</td></tr>
<tr><td>1902–6</td><td>Becomes pupil-teacher at British School at Eastwood; begins writing The White Peacock and poems. Engaged to Jessie Chambers.</td></tr>
<tr><td>1906–8</td><td>Attends Nottingham University College, taking the teacher's certificate course.</td></tr>
<tr><td>1908–11</td><td>Teaches at the Davidson Road Boy's School; Jessie Chambers sends some of his poems to Ford Madox Hueffer's English Review, where Lawrence's poetry is first published in the November 1909 issue of English Review. Friendship with Helen Corke, a schoolteacher.</td></tr>
<tr><td>1910</td><td>Starts writing The Trespasser; engagement with Jessie broken off; starts writing Paul Morel (to become Sons and Lovers). His mother dies of cancer, December 10.</td></tr>
<tr><td>1911</td><td>His first novel, The White Peacock, is published by Heinemann in January.</td></tr>
<tr><td>1912</td><td>Falls ill and gives up teaching. Introduced to Frieda von Richthofen Weekley, the thirty-two-year-old wife of his former French professor at University College, Nottingham. The Trespasser published in May. Lawrence</td></tr>
</table>

and Frieda travel together in Germany and Italy. Finishes *Sons and Lovers*; writes plays, stories, and poems.

1913   *Sons and Lovers* published in May. Begins *The Insurrection of Miss Houghton* (to become *The Lost Girl*). Works on draft of *The Sisters* (to become *Women in Love* and *The Rainbow*); writes tales published as *The Prussian Officer* (1914). Meets John Middleton Murry.

1914   Frieda divorces Weekley and marries Lawrence. *Study of Thomas Hardy* written, and work continues on *The Sisters*.

1915   *The Rainbow* published in September, suppressed for "indecency" in November. Writes *The Gown*.

1916   Lives in Cornwall; finishes writing *Women in Love*.

1917   Denied passport to U.S.; rejected as medically unfit for military service; expelled by military from Cornwall on suspicion of spying.

1918   Drafts *Movements in European Literature*, the play *Touch and Go*, and *The Fox*.

1919   Writes tales published as *England, My England*; drafts *Aaron's Rod*; returns to Continent: Florence, Capri, Taormina.

1920   *Women in Love* is privately printed in New York. Completes and publishes *The Lost Girl*; writes *Birds, Beasts and Flowers*, *Psychoanalysis and the Unconscious* (1921), and a novel, *Mr. Noon*.

1921   Writes *Fantasia of the Unconscious* (1922), *The Captain's Doll*, and *The Ladybird*.

1922   Visits Ceylon and Australia, where he writes most of *Kangaroo*. *Aaron's Rod* published in April. Takes up residence in Taos, New Mexico.

1923   Completes and publishes *Birds, Beasts and Flowers*; *Kangaroo* published; begins work on *The Plumed Serpent*. Visits Mexico and Europe.

1924   Writes *Mornings in Mexico* (1927), *St. Mawr* (1925), and the tales *The Princess* and *The Woman Who Rode Away*.

1925   Completes *The Plumed Serpent* and the play *David St. Mawr* published.

1926   *The Plumed Serpent* published in January. Takes up residence near Florence. Begins writing *Lady Chatterley's Lover*.

1927   Begins work on *Escaped Cock* (published as *The Man Who Died* and *Etruscan Places* [1932]).

1928 Completes *Lady Chatterley's Lover*, published first in Florence, though numerous pirated editions appear in England. Resides in South of France. Postal authorities seize manuscript of *Pansies*. Completes *The Man Who Died* (1929).

1929 Police raid exhibition of Lawrence's paintings at the Warren Gallery, London (July). Writes *More Pansies, Pornography and Obscenity, Apocalypse,* and *Nettles*.

1930 Dies of tuberculosis at a sanatorium near Antibes, France, on March 2.

1960 Penguin Books publishes unexpurgated *Lady Chatterley's Lover* in England and is prosecuted under the Obscene Publications Act. After a celebrated trial, Penguin wins.

Contributors

HAROLD BLOOM, Sterling Professor of the Humanities at Yale University, is the author of *The Anxiety of Influence, Poetry and Repression*, and many other volumes of literary criticism. His forthcoming study, *Freud: Transference and Authority*, attempts a full-scale reading of all of Freud's major writings. A MacArthur Prize Fellow, he is general editor of five series of literary criticism published by Chelsea House. During 1987–88, he served as Charles Eliot Norton Professor of Poetry at Harvard University.

H. M. DALESKI, Professor of English Literature at the Hebrew University of Jerusalem, is the author of *The Forked Flame: A Study of D. H. Lawrence, Dickens and the Art of Analogy*, and *Joseph Conrad: The Way of Dispossession*.

PETER K. GARRETT teaches English at the University of Illinois. He is the author of *Scene and Symbol from George Eliot to James Joyce* and *The Victorian Multiplot Novel: Studies in Dialogical Form*.

ROBERT L. CASERIO is Associate Professor of English at the University of Utah. He is the author of *Plot, Story and the Novel: From Dickens and Poe to the Modern Period*.

JOHN WORTHEN, who teaches English at the University College of Wales, Swansea, is the author of *D. H. Lawrence and the Idea of the Novel*. He is the editor of *"The Prussian Officer" and Other Stories* and *Women in Love*, both volumes in the Cambridge Edition of the Works of D. H. Lawrence.

GAVRIEL BEN-EPHRAIM teaches at Tel Aviv University and is the author of *The Moon's Dominion: Narrative Dichotomy and Female Dominance in Lawrence's Earlier Novels*.

BARUCH HOCHMAN teaches at Hebrew University. He is the author of *The Fiction of S. Y. Agnon*, *Character in Literature*, and *Another Ego: The Changing View of Self and Society in the Work of D. H. Lawrence*.

PHILIP M. WEINSTEIN teaches at Swarthmore College. His most recent book is *The Semantics of Desire: The Changing Roles of Identity from Dickens to Joyce*.

MARIA DiBATTISTA is Associate Professor of English at Princeton University. She is the author of *Virginia Woolf's Major Novels*.

Bibliography

Albright, Daniel. *Personality and Impersonality: Lawrence, Woolf, and Mann.* Chicago: University of Chicago Press, 1978.

Alldrit, Keith. *The Visual Imagination of D. H. Lawrence.* Evanston, Ill.: Northwestern University Press, 1971.

Balbert, Peter, and Phillip L. Marcus, eds. *D. H. Lawrence: A Centenary Consideration.* Ithaca, N.Y.: Cornell University Press, 1985.

Bedient, Calvin. *Architects of the Self: George Eliot, D. H. Lawrence, and E. M. Forster.* Berkeley: University of California Press, 1972.

Bersani, Leo. *A Future for Astyanax: Character and Desire in Literature.* London: Marion Boyars, 1978.

Blanchard, Lydia. "*Women in Love*: Mourning Becomes Narcissism." *Mosaic* 15, no. 1 (Winter 1982): 105–18.

Cavitch, David, *D. H. Lawrence and the New World.* New York: Oxford University Press, 1969.

Clark, L. D. *The Minoan Distance: The Symbolism of Travel in D. H. Lawrence.* Tucson: University of Arizona Press, 1980.

Clarke, Colin. *River of Dissolution: D. H. Lawrence and English Romanticism.* New York: Barnes & Noble, 1969.

Cockshut, A. O. J. *Man and Woman: A Study of Love in the Novel, 1740–1940.* New York: Oxford University Press, 1978.

The D. H. Lawrence Review, 1968–.

Delany, Paul. *D. H. Lawrence's Nightmare: The Writer and His Circle in the Years of the Great War.* New York: Basic, 1978.

Delavenay, Emile. *D. H. Lawrence and Edward Carpenter: A Study in Edwardian Transition.* New York: Taplinger, 1971.

———. *D. H. Lawrence, The Man and His Work: The Formative Years, 1885–1919.* Translated by Katherine M. Delavenay. London: Heinemann, 1972.

Dervin, Daniel. *A Strange Sapience: The Creative Imagination of D. H. Lawrence.* Amherst: University of Massachusetts Press, 1984.

DiGaetani, John Louis. *Richard Wagner and the Modern British Novel.* London and Toronto: Associated University Presses, 1978.

Dix, Carol. *D. H. Lawrence and Women.* London: Macmillan, 1980.

Friedman, Alan. *The Turn of the Novel.* New York: Oxford University Press, 1966.

Gindin, James. *Harvest of a Quiet Eye: The Novel of Compassion*. Bloomington: Indiana University Press, 1971.

Goodheart, Eugene. *The Utopian Vision of D. H. Lawrence*. Chicago: University of Chicago Press, 1963.

Gregory, Horace. *Pilgrim of the Apocalypse*. New York: Viking, 1933.

Hardy, Barbara. *The Appropriate Form: An Essay on the Novel*. London: Athlone, 1964.

Harper, Howard M., Jr. "*Fantasia* and the Psychodynamics of *Women in Love*." In *The Classic British Novel*, edited by Howard M. Harper, Jr. and Charles Edge. Athens: University of Georgia Press, 1972.

Hochman, Baruch. *Another Ego: The Changing View of Self and Society in the Work of D. H. Lawrence*. Columbia: University of South Carolina Press, 1970.

Hoffman, Frederick, J., and Harry T. Moore, eds. *The Achievement of D. H. Lawrence*. Norman: University of Oklahoma Press, 1953.

Kalnins, Mara, ed. *D. H. Lawrence: Centenary Essays*. Bristol, England: Bristol Classical Press, 1986.

Kermode, Frank. "D. H. Lawrence and the Apocalyptic Types." *Critical Quarterly* 10 (Spring 1968): 14–38.

Kiely, Robert. *Beyond Egotism: The Fiction of James Joyce, Virginia Woolf, and D. H. Lawrence*. Cambridge: Harvard University Press, 1980.

Krieger, Murray. *The Tragic Vision*. New York: Holt, Rinehart & Winston, 1960.

Langbaum, Robert. *The Mysteries of Identity: A Theme in Modern Literature*. New York: Oxford University Press, 1977.

Leavis, F. R. *D. H. Lawrence: Novelist*. New York: Knopf, 1956.

———. *Thought, Words, and Creativity: Art and Thought in Lawrence*. New York: Oxford University Press, 1976.

Lerner, Laurence. *The Truthtellers: Jane Austen, George Eliot, and D. H. Lawrence*. New York: Schocken, 1967.

MacLeod, Sheila. *Lawrence's Men and Women*. London: Heinemann, 1985.

Mailer, Norman. "The Prisoner of Sex." *Harper's Magazine*, March 1971: 41–92.

Marković, Vida E. *The Changing Face: Disintegration of Personality in the Twentieth Century British Novel, 1900–1950*. Carbondale: Southern Illinois University Press, 1970.

Martin, W. R. " 'Freedom Together' in *Women in Love*." *English Studies in Africa* 8 (1965): 111–20.

Meyers, Jeffrey. "*D. H. Lawrence and Homosexuality*." *London Magazine* 13 no. 4 (1973): 68–93.

Miles, Rosalind. *The Fiction of Sex: Themes and Functions of Sex Difference in the Modern Novel*. London: Vision Press, 1974.

Miko, Stephen J. *Toward* Women in Love. New Haven: Yale University Press, 1971.

———, ed. *Twentieth Century Interpretations of* Women in Love. Englewood Cliffs, N.J.: Prentice-Hall, 1969.

Miller, D. A. *Narrative and Its Discontents: Problems of Closure in the Traditional Novel*. Princeton: Princeton University Press, 1981.

Moore, Harry T., ed. *The Collected Letters of D. H. Lawrence*. 2 vols. New York: Viking, 1962.

———. *A D. H. Lawrence Miscellany*. Carbondale: Southern Illinois University Press, 1959.

Moynahan, Julian. *The Deed of Life: The Novels and Tales of D. H. Lawrence.* Princeton: Princeton University Press, 1963.

New, Peter. *Fiction and Purpose in* Utopia, Rasselas, The Mill on the Floss, *and* Women in Love. London: Macmillan, 1985.

Nixon, Cornelia. *Lawrence's Leadership Politics and the Turn against Women.* Berkeley: University of California Press, 1986.

Oates, Joyce Carol. "Lawrence's Götterdämmerung: The Tragic Vision of *Women in Love.*" *Critical Inquiry* 4 (Spring 1978): 559–78.

Partlow, Robert B., and Harry T. Moore, eds. *D. H. Lawrence: The Man Who Lived.* Carbondale: Southern Illinois University Press, 1980.

Pinion, F. B. *A D. H. Lawrence Companion.* London: Macmillan, 1978.

Ragussis, Michael. *The Subterfuge of Art: Language and the Romantic Tradition.* Baltimore: The Johns Hopkins University Press, 1978.

Sagar, Keith. *The Art of D. H. Lawrence.* Cambridge: Cambridge University Press, 1966.

———. *D. H. Lawrence: Life into Art.* Athens: University of Georgia Press, 1985.

Sanders, Scott. *D. H. Lawrence: The World of the Major Novels.* New York: Viking, 1973.

Scheckner, Peter. *Class, Politics, and the Individual.* London and Toronto: Associated University Presses, 1985.

Schneider, Daniel J. *D. H. Lawrence: The Artist as Psychologist.* Kansas City: University Press of Kansas, 1984.

———. *D. H. Lawrence: The Consciousness of D. H. Lawrence.* Kansas City: University Press of Kansas, 1986.

Schorer, Mark. *The World We Imagine.* New York: Farrar, Straus & Giroux, 1968.

Smith, Anne, ed. *Lawrence and Women.* London: Vision Press, 1978.

Spender, Stephen, ed. *D. H. Lawrence: Novelist, Poet, and Prophet.* London: Weidenfield & Nicolson, 1973.

Spilka, Mark. *A Collection of Criticial Essays.* Englewood Cliffs, N.J.: Prentice-Hall, 1963.

———. *The Love Ethic of D. H. Lawrence.* Bloomington: Indiana University Press, 1955.

Stoll, John E. *The Novels of D. H. Lawrence: A Search for Integration.* Columbia: University of Missouri Press, 1971.

Tomlinson, T. B. *The English Middle-Class Novel.* London: Macmillan, 1976.

Torgovnick, Marianna. "Closure and the Shape of Fictions: The Example of *Women in Love.*" In *The Study of Time IV,* edited by J. T. Fraser, et al. New York: Springer-Verlag, 1981.

———. *The Visual Arts, Pictorialism, and the Novel: James, Lawrence, and Woolf.* Princeton: Princeton University Press, 1985.

Vivas, Eliseo. "The Substance of *Women in Love.*" *The Sewanee Review* 66 (Autumn 1958): 588–632.

Williams, Raymond. *The English Novel from Dickens to Lawrence.* London: Chatto & Windus, 1970.

Acknowledgments

"Two in One: The Second Period" by H. M. Daleski from *The Forked Flame: A Study of D. H. Lawrence* by H. M. Daleski, © 1965 by H.M. Dalseki. Reprinted by permission.

"The Revelation of the Unconscious" by Peter K. Garrett from *Scene and Symbol from George Eliot to James Joyce: Studies in Changing Fictional Mode* by Peter K. Garrett, © 1969 by Yale University. Reprinted by permission of Yale University Press.

"The Family Plot" (originally entitled "The Family Plot: Conrad, Joyce, Lawrence, Woolf, and Faulkner") by Robert L. Caserio from *Plot, Story and the Novel: From Dickens and Poe to the Modern Period* by Robert L. Caserio, © 1979 by Princeton University Press. Reprinted by permission of Princeton University Press.

"*Women in Love*: The Ideology of Society" (originally entitled "*Women in Love*") by John Worthen from *D. H. Lawrence and the Idea of the Novel* by John Worthen, © 1979 by John Worthen. Reprinted by permission of the author, Macmillan Press, London and Basingstoke and Barnes & Noble Books, Totowa, New Jersey.

"The Teller Reasserted: Exercisings of the Will in *Women in Love*" by Gavriel Ben-Ephraim from *The Moon Dominion: Narrative Dichotomy and Female Dominance in Lawrence's Earlier Novels* by Gavriel Ben-Ephraim, © 1981 by Associated University Presses, Inc. Reprinted by permission of Associated University Presses, Inc.

"On the Shape the Self Takes" (originally entitled "On the Shape of the Self Takes: Henry James to D. H. Lawrence") by Baruch Hochman from *The Test of Character: From the Victorian Novel to the Modern* by Baruch Hochman, © 1983 by Associated University Press, Inc. Reprinted by permission of Associated University Press, Inc.

"The Trembling Instability of *Women in Love*" by Philip M. Weinstein from *The Semantics of Desire: Changing Models of Identity from Dickens to Joyce* by Philip M. Weinstein, © 1984 by Princeton University Press. Reprinted by permission of Princeton University Press.

"*Women in Love*: D. H. Lawrence's Judgment Book" by Maria DiBattista from *D. H. Lawrence: A Centenary Consideration*, edited by Peter Balbert and Philip L. Marcus, © 1985 by Cornell University Press. Reprinted by permission of Cornell University Press.

Index